BRIDGING WORLDS

Bridging Worlds

Unlocking the Secrets of Intuitive Animal Communication

Alex Andersen

Published by Game Changer Publishing

Paperback ISBN: 978-1-964811-29-1
Hardcover ISBN: 978-1-964811-30-7
Digital ISBN: 978-1-964811-31-4

GAME CHANGER
PUBLISHING

www.GameChangerPublishing.com

DEDICATION

To my beloved animals and the natural world, your presence has been a guiding light in my life. You have shaped who I am and helped me grow my skills with your gentle wisdom and unwavering service. Every moment spent with you has been a lesson in patience, love, and understanding.

To my husband, Rob, writing this section of the dedication has been the most challenging part of this entire book. How could I possibly encapsulate the depth of my gratitude and joy for you in just a few short words? Your unwavering support and belief in me have served as my anchor through everything. Your ability to stand by my side as both my home base and my greatest adventure partner is a testament to the strength of our bond. Your love has carried me through every high and low. I am infinitely grateful for your presence, your kindness, and the countless ways you encourage me to pursue my dreams. Thank you for being the incredible person you are; your impact on my life is immeasurable.

To my family and friends, your encouragement and faith in me have been a constant source of strength. Going public with this type of work brings its own set of challenges; it is easy to get caught up in worries about how others might perceive me, how society might react, and how it could impact us all. It is not lost on me how blessed I am to have you all in my life, providing continuous, unquestionable support and celebration as we move the needle forward on this mission of connection. You were my first to experience connection in this world, and I love you endlessly.

To my Aunt Nichol, your influence in my life extended far beyond those first horse lessons at the age of 11 that you and Uncle Ian so kindly gifted me. You not only ignited my passion for horses, but you also nurtured my relationship with them and with nature itself. I fondly remember the joyful trail rides you took me on, where the world faded away, and I found a profound connection with the beauty of the outdoors and the gentle spirits of the horses. Those moments were not just about riding; they were transformative experiences that deepened my bond with nature. Though you are no longer with us, your presence remains in every ride through sunlit mountains, every rustle of the wind through the trees, and every breath taken with the horses. Your presence in my life has left an unforgettable imprint on my heart, reminding me that, even in your absence, your love and hilarious sense of humor continue to guide us all on this journey. Thank you for being the light that brightly illuminates our memories, eternally inspiring us to cherish our connection with animals, nature, and each other.

With all my heart, I extend my deepest gratitude to each of you. This book is a reflection of the unconditional love and support that surrounds me.

With deepest gratitude,
Alex Andersen

Read This First

Thank you for purchasing and reading my book! As a token of my appreciation, I'm excited to offer you a complimentary training. This training will guide you through the steps to connect with animals, helping you deepen your understanding and bond with them.

Enjoy this journey, and I look forward to supporting you along the way!

Scan the QR Code Here:

SCAN ME!

Bridging Worlds

Unlocking the Secrets of Intuitive
Animal Communication

Alex Andersen

GC GAME CHANGER PUBLISHING

www.GameChangerPublishing.com

Table of Contents

Introduction

I am Alex Andersen, and I extend my hand to you as a bridge between worlds. Once an agent in the bustling world of real estate and human coaching, with eight years under my belt, I have now embraced the call of the wild—a call that took hold of my heart during the stillness of 2020's global pause but began years earlier. My spiritual awakening and curiosity began in my early 20s when I had a few limited experiences with mediumship. I had hired mediums before, but it wasn't until I had an experience with my horse that I thought I might be able to learn it.

I had just brought in a half-ton bale of hay into my horses' dry pasture for them to free feed on, and we hadn't yet put a net over it for slow-feeding purposes. Standing by the fence for a break, my mom beside me, we watched the quiet rhythm of farm life unfold until an unexpected visitor approached.

As Zip, my spirited sorrel Arabian horse, walked toward us, something about him immediately set off alarms in my heart. I noticed an abnormal stream of mucus trailing from his nostrils, and his usually proud head drooped sorrowfully low. His steps were sluggish, each one seemingly an effort, painting a picture of lethargy. My eyes scanned him up and down, searching for clues to his distress, when suddenly, a loud, internal cry interrupted my thoughts: "I can't breathe!" It was as clear and jarring as if I had screamed at myself, a telepathic plea for help that left no room for doubt. Zip was choking.

A choking horse doesn't appear as frantic as one might expect, and the condition isn't obvious, especially to those unfamiliar with the condition. Despite my years of experience with horses, this was a first for me. Without hesitation, I reached for my phone and, with trembling hands, called the vet. My vet's voice, calm and reassuring, informed me that this was often not a cause for panic, as many horses find their way through such episodes on their own. However, the "better safe than sorry" mantra that has always guided me prompted me to take no chances. My aunt Nichol came to the rescue as she trailered Zip, and we took him to the veterinary clinic, where he received the care he needed to clear the blockage. Zip was perfectly fine and recovered fully, but the episode left a lasting mark on me.

The incident stirred deep questions within me. Had I truly received a telepathic message from Zip in his moment of need? And if so, could I somehow harness this connection at will? It was a revelation too profound to dismiss yet too personal, too enigmatic, to share openly. I kept the experience close to my chest, only sharing it with a few close people, but as life on the farm marched on, I held a secret wonderment at the possible depths of connection between human and horse.

Despite the profound and somewhat mystical experience with Zip, which planted the seed for depths of connection I had yet to fully understand, life, with its relentless pace and demands, called me back. The event, though unforgettable, was gently placed on the back burner of my mind as I returned to the rhythm of my daily existence.

I was deeply engrossed in the world of real estate and entrepreneurship, a path I had been navigating with unwavering dedication for over eight years. My commitment and passion for this field were recognized, and I found myself mentoring new agents within my brokerage, sharing insights, and guiding budding careers while still working with my own private clients. Despite my achievements and the satisfaction they brought, I felt this sense of restlessness that took my attention beyond the transactions and negotiations of real estate.

I could sense it, a missing piece to my puzzle, evoking a subtle dissatisfaction that nudged me into uncharted territories.

When I heard this knock to explore the animal communication world, it wasn't just a call to the door but a deeper calling aligned with my passion for understanding and enhancing the human mind. My expertise spans real estate, neurolinguistics, and hypnotherapy, all rooted in a lifelong fascination with psychology and the brain's incredible potential. This pursuit of mental mastery, aimed at helping people harness their minds for greater fulfillment and achievement, has been a guiding force in my life.

My exploration into the mind's capabilities didn't stop with humans; it also extended to animals, fueled by my love for them and fascination with therapeutic modalities. The idea that the same principles could foster healing and understanding across species was both a revelation and a challenge that I eagerly embraced.

Throughout most of my life, I've believed in animal communication in the sense that we can send and receive energetic information, but I wasn't yet convinced that it was a skill available to everyone. My spiritual and professional journeys unveiled its accessibility to all. This realization marked a thrilling new chapter in my mission to bridge the gap between human and animal minds, opening doors to untapped possibilities of mutual growth and healing.

I must confess that my initial feelings about becoming an animal communicator were a mix of curiosity and skepticism. It seemed to me that the ability to communicate with animals was a special gift some possessed naturally while others did not. I never envisioned myself as one who could ever claim to be any kind of expert in the field. However, my background in understanding the intricacies of the human mind, particularly the unconscious, inspired me to explore the possibility of becoming an animal communicator.

The 2020 lockdown found me immersed in YouTube videos of animal communicators, sparking a dream I had never dared to entertain. Doubts surfaced as quickly as desire and intrigue—the kind of self-questioning that whispers, *You can't do this.* I immediately challenged the thought. Why shouldn't I pursue this? If it was true that anyone could learn and I was committed to the path, what stood in the way of success? This realization ignited a newfound passion within me, pushing me to enroll in an animal communication course.

However, an interesting shift occurred upon starting the course. As I dove into the first lesson, I realized the material wasn't revealing anything unknown to me. Rather than finding new knowledge, I discovered that I was searching for a unique approach to harnessing this skill.

I was interested in unraveling the workings of the mind, not merely tapping into the body's energy. I wanted to integrate various disciplines to train both mind and body more effectively. Drawing upon my knowledge of neuro-programming, the interaction between the unconscious and conscious minds, and hypnotherapy principles, I set out to develop a unique methodology. This approach was designed to accelerate the mastery of these skills.

Within the first six months of this budding exploration, I started offering free sessions to garner experience and obtain feedback on my accuracy and technique. My commitment to refining my skills quickly paid off, leading to an expanding practice and a growing list of clients. My background proved particularly advantageous in coaching animals through challenging times, employing creative strategies that yielded swift, positive outcomes. This success didn't go unnoticed, and my client base began to expand further by word of mouth. I took to sharing my insights and experiences slowly online and with a small audience at the time, as I was nervous about what people would think and how it would affect my real estate business.

By the time I got serious about promoting my services online, I'd had a solid year of working with animals behind the scenes. I began to share success stories, which added significant value for my audience and, in turn, spurred the growth of my online presence. Only a year after taking my marketing seriously, I found myself with a three-year client waitlist—a development that was as surprising as it was gratifying.

For someone who'd initially known little about animal communication, this was no small feat. Far from being a natural-born communicator with animals, recognized for such talents from a young age, I was merely someone deeply passionate about animals and their well-being. This love for animals guided me toward a wholly unexpected career path, one where my desire to see them heal transformed into a professional calling.

Not long after establishing my practice, I ventured into teaching, driven by the growing demand for these services and the conviction that there is ample opportunity for everyone in this field. Teaching aligns with my goal to demystify animal communication, making it more accepted and accessible. I see this work as deeply scientific and practical, capable of delivering significant outcomes for those who seek it. My vision is to foster a society of empowered individuals who recognize and cultivate their inherent abilities rather than solely relying on others.

After nearly two years of teaching, I had guided hundreds of students and conducted over six hundred private sessions. Our collective mission is flourishing, building a community of animal enthusiasts skilled in communication, thereby revolutionizing the industry with fresh insights into animal connection. This book is more than just a read; it's an open invitation to engage in an ancient conversation between humans and animals, welcoming anyone drawn to deepening their bond with our animal friends and the world around us.

I felt compelled to write this book because I know there are many out there like me: People who believe that there's more than meets the eye when it comes to the world of animal communication and who hold the conviction that a deeper vein of understanding and connectivity exists, just waiting to be tapped. This book is an homage to you, the animal lovers and spiritual seekers who strive not just to coexist with our furry, feathery, and scaly companions but to understand them, to speak to and to hear them, transcending the traditional boundaries of interspecies communication.

My years of dedication to studying animal behavior, along with cultivating a mindfulness practice tuned into the subtle frequencies of life, have provided me with insights that I am eager to share with you. Like any language, the language of animals is complex and nuanced, and through dedication and practice, it can be comprehended and spoken. Here, I have distilled my experiences and learnings, offering them as a guide to help you forge your path to profound communication with the creatures with whom we share our lives and our planet.

As you read through the chapters, I'll share stories from my animal communication sessions over the years. Some will use real names, while others will have their names changed to respect privacy. However, all of them are based on real events, conversations, and results.

In these pages, you will uncover practical advice and exercises designed to fine-tune your observation skills, hone your intuitive faculties, and establish a deeper, more empathetic relationship with animals. You will not only learn to listen to but understand the whispered wisdom that each creature imparts and respect the unique energy and spirit they embody. My hope is that as you turn each page, you nurture a profound appreciation for the world's symphony of silent speech and that, by the end of your reading, you emerge not as a mere observer of nature but as an integral participant in its chorus. The connection you've always felt with animals will deepen into an active, meaningful dialogue.

So, with hearts wide open to the possibilities that lie ahead, we venture into the first chapter, where we'll explore the basic energetics of life, the fundamental frequencies that form the basis of all communication, setting the stage for the odyssey to come. Together, we will learn to listen and to speak, and in doing so, we will discover a kinship with the animal kingdom that transcends all barriers, a kindred connection from heart to heart, soul to soul, and life to life. Your journey into the heart of animal communication begins now.

CHAPTER 1

Understanding Energetics and Intuition

E nergy permeates both the human body and the surrounding environment, manifesting in diverse forms and possessing measurable vibrational frequencies that influence every aspect of our reality. In the human body, energy flows through various channels, influencing physical, emotional, and mental states, while in the environment, it plays a vital role in shaping ecosystems and sustaining life. Dr. Masaru Emoto's innovative research on water crystals delves into the profound impact of energy on our surroundings through vibrational frequencies, unveiling the intricate relationship between energy and matter.

Dr. Masaru Emoto hypothesized that human consciousness, through words, thoughts, emotions, and intentions, can affect the molecular structure of water. In his experiments, he exposed distilled water to various verbal and written stimuli, froze it, and examined the crystals formed under a microscope. According to his findings and captivating photographic evidence, positive words and intentions led to aesthetically pleasing crystal formations, while negative words and intentions resulted in disordered or unattractive crystal structures. His work suggests an interconnectedness between human emotional energy and the physical world, offering tangible evidence of how the vibrational frequency of words and thoughts can directly influence the structure of water. Considering that humans are 60–75% water, dogs up to 70% water, and cats 60–70% water, these findings are pretty significant!

Additionally and intriguingly, Dr. Masaru Emoto's research paved the way to expanding our understanding of telepathy—the direct transfer of information between minds through energetic means. His notable experiment with Tokyo's tap water serves as a compelling example. In this experiment, he had five hundred people remotely send a "chi of love" to the city's tap water, resulting yet again in a beautiful crystalized shape once frozen. This demonstrated the tangible effects of collective human intention, emotions, and energetic focus on the molecular structure of water.

In traditional Chinese culture and medicine, "chi" is the vital life force energy believed to flow through all living beings, essential for maintaining health and wellness. In this context, a "chi of love" signifies the idea that positive intentions like love and kindness can be sent remotely to water, transmitting loving life force energy. Similar terminology describing the belief of vital life force energy can be found in many cultures and beliefs around the world. Other similar terms include Ki (Japanese), Prana (Sanskrit - referring to life-sustaining energy), Mana (Polynesian - referring to divine spiritual power and life force energy), etc. It is what German physician Franz Anton Mesmer also described as magnetic fluid in the late 1700s.

This experiment not only underlines the potential impact of human energy and intentionality on the physical world but also opens the door to considering how much energetic transference can facilitate communication or influence at a quantum level. The possibility of energetic information transference invites us to reconsider the boundaries of communication, hinting at the vast, untapped potential of the mind and the underlying connectedness of all things.

Understanding these vibrational frequencies is crucial for nonverbal psychic animal communication. As animals are predominantly composed of water, like humans, they are attuned to the vibrational energies of their environment—even more so than humans! This knowledge is necessary to understand how skilled people connect with animals on a deeper level through telepathic animal communication, transcending more traditional verbal language barriers. Animals, like humans, emit and interpret energy by being attuned to the energetic frequencies that permeate their surroundings. They truly are experts in effortlessly understanding the world of telepathy, energy, and frequencies. By working the telepathic muscles of the mind and tapping into these vibrations, we, too, can begin to communicate and connect with them on this level.

Energy serves as a bridge between different forms of life, enabling deeper understanding and communication that transcend the limitations of verbal expression. Through this lens, the role of energy and nonverbal psychic animal communication becomes a compelling testament to the interconnectedness of all living beings. Energy permeates every aspect of our reality, from the sustenance of life to the dynamics of human emotions and interactions. The pivotal question that arises is not whether energy exists and if we can communicate through it, but rather, how attuned we are to its influence.

Jumping into the exploration of energy attunement is like unlocking a secret pathway to our intuition, consciousness, and connection with everything around us. Before we can master this skill, it's important to get acquainted with the primary tool at our disposal: ourselves. Think of it like learning to drive. You wouldn't just hop into a car and speed off without knowing the basics. You start with understanding where the breaks are, how to steer, and how to signal turns.

We're taking that same foundational approach, but instead of navigating roads, we're navigating the realms of telepathic communication and intuitive skills. This is your introductory guide to the inner mechanics of your mind, setting the stage for an exciting journey to enhancing your natural abilities.

The Three Minds

To unlock the secrets of the mind's power, we turn our focus to the three key players that make it all happen: the unconscious mind, the conscious mind, and the higher-conscious mind. Understanding how these three operate is like finding the ultimate cheat code for translating incoming telepathic and energetic information.

To really see the full picture, we'll start with the basics of how our bodies process information. Various studies report different figures, but it is commonly stated that the mind takes in as much as 11 million bits per second of information at a time through our five senses; this is also known as our reticular activating system. Some studies have shown more. Either way, imagine trying to process all that at once! It would be like plugging a toaster into a power plant—total overload. Rather than tackling all that information head-on, the mind and body break it down into manageable, bite-sized chunks that can be more easily understood and used.

Imagine the world around us as a constant stream of data and sensations flooding in through the gateways of our five senses: we see (visual), we hear (auditory), we feel (kinesthetic), we smell (olfactory), and we taste (gustatory). This information is still too vast for us to process in its entirety. Thus, our mind steps in as a masterful curator to break down this sensory data further.

The mind's filtering process is methodical and discerning, governed by a set of internal criteria. It selectively deletes, distorts, and generalizes sensory input based on our unique language, memories, values, beliefs, experiences, and meta programs that run in the background of our psyche.

Meta programs might metaphorically be described as the mental software of our minds, guiding us in interpreting the world. They are mental filters that shape how we perceive and respond to the world around us, influencing preferences, decision-making, and communication styles.

At this point, you might be thinking, *That's quite a sophisticated operation,* and you'd be right. However, the mind doesn't stop there. With the heavy lifting done by these processes, what emerges is an internal representation of the information—our personalized, internal version of reality. This internal snapshot shapes our current state of mind or being, which, in turn, influences our physiology and creates our behaviors. These behaviors, stemming from our internal representations, are expressed outwardly, shaping the results we experience in our lives. It's a profound cycle where the internal and external continuously dance, each influencing the other in ways both subtle and significant. We truly do create our reality.

This also explains why, if a group of people witness the same car accident, their accounts to the responding officer will vary. Each person will attempt to reconstruct the event, but their mind will process the incident in a distinct manner. Similarly, when multiple animal communicators engage with the same animal and pose identical questions, they can end up with the same general consensus of information, yet the details will differ due to the unique processing of each communicator's mind.

Now that we've peeled back the layers of the fascinating diversity within our inner worlds, you've seen how we all view things through our own unique lenses. This variety in perception makes our interactions and understanding of the world richer. To build on this and give you a clearer picture of how intuition works, we're going to look at the three levels of the mind: the unconscious, conscious, and higher-conscious minds. Grasping these three aspects will enable you to understand how intuition leads us and how you can deliberately access and enhance your ability to use it.

The Unconscious Mind

The unconscious mind is a powerful force that does much more than keep our bodies alive—and even that alone is pretty incredible! Science tells us that a whopping 95% of our brain activity happens at the unconscious level. This means that most of what we decide, do, feel, and act on comes from a place that most of us are not even aware of.

The development of the unconscious mind begins during the brain's development while we're in the womb. From the moment we're born until the age of seven or eight (when the conscious mind kicks in), the unconscious is essentially in charge, soaking up everything in our environment like a sponge. This is because the critical faculty of our conscious mind is wide open; you might think of it as the conscious mind just being along for the ride in this phase of life. During these early years, the unconscious mind, which is symbolic in nature and interprets everything literally, is the mastermind behind our cognitive processes, meticulously recording incoming information from our environment.

Before the conscious mind begins to engage, the unconscious mind is all there really is. It captures and stores all of our experiences, the words we hear, the lessons we learn, the emotions we feel, and more. This stage is crucial because it is when the foundation of our mental and emotional blueprint is laid out, including the filters we discussed earlier, through which we take in and process information. This makes up the bulk of that 95% of unconscious brain activity.

Throughout our lives, the unconscious molds our perception of the world, ideally absorbing new information to promote inner growth, yet it still drives our habits and deep-seated beliefs without us even realizing it. It uses all of the data it's collected to influence how we connect with others and respond emotionally, operating on a level that words almost can't capture. It can learn lots of things all at one time, but it does so experientially. Additionally, it does not immediately process negatives. If I were to tell you, "Don't think about a blue tree," you'd likely immediately think of a blue tree.

Combining these concepts, consider what happens when you warn a child, "Don't touch that stove. It's hot." That warning might actually pique their curiosity as it inadvertently plants the idea of touching the stove. If the child does touch the stove, their unconscious mind learns several things at once: stoves can be hot, heat can cause physical burns, burns are painful, and touching hot stoves should be avoided.

Despite the unconscious mind performing a myriad of functions and operating beyond our direct awareness, its most profound attribute is its ability to be reprogrammed. For example, this is what makes hypnotherapy so effective, with a success rate of over 93%. Through techniques like hypnotherapy, a person is guided into a state where their brainwaves slow down, the conscious mind takes a back seat, and the unconscious mind can more easily make positive changes. It's an approach that goes straight to where our deepest patterns and beliefs are stored, offering a powerful pathway to personal growth and healing.

What's more, the unconscious mind might be the key to understanding psychic phenomena, as it is the ruler of our intuitive connection. When we pick up intuitive, psychic, or telepathic signals, it's our unconscious mind that processes this information. The challenge arises when our conscious mind doubts or dismisses these insights as false. Our unconscious mind is already equipped to telepathically communicate with animals. I often tell my students, "Your unconscious mind already knows how; we just have to convince it that it *can*."

Adding to this, the unique developmental stage of children, who are primarily in an unconscious state until around the age of seven or eight, sheds light on their heightened capacity for psychic phenomena. This period in their lives is characterized by a more fluid connection to the unconscious mind, allowing them to have the full range of their natural intuitive skills and even "see" relatives who have passed, recall past life experiences, and communicate intuitively with animals. During this phase of life, natural psychic abilities can be the most pronounced.

However, as the conscious mind begins to assert, these abilities often fade. The emerging conscious mind filters and gradually sidelines these psychic abilities as it starts to rationalize things, and the child begins to mold themselves into their environment and take on certain social norms as they enter their "modeling" phase.

The Conscious Mind

The conscious mind represents our thoughtful, rational, and logical mental processes. Central to its function is setting goals and formulating plans to achieve them. Unlike the unconscious mind, which can learn many things all at once, the conscious mind learns sequentially, taking in one piece of data at a time. It's the driver behind our cognitive learning, encompassing all our thinking and rational activities.

Additionally, the conscious mind controls our voluntary movements. For example, the decision to reach out and pick up a cup of coffee involves a conscious thought process, translating intention into action. Or, as I will show you later in this book, the conscious mind will decide to collaborate with the unconscious mind, taking deliberate steps to practice and enhance intuitive animal communication. This part of our mind is perpetually inquisitive, asking questions like "why" and seeking to understand the answers more analytically. In contrast, the unconscious mind operates on an instinctual level, often knowing the answer without the need for step-by-step reasoning. When faced with the answer, it's the conscious mind's role to analyze and make sense of it, piecing together information that aligns with our understanding and logical structures.

In the realm of developing intuitive skills, the conscious mind plays a crucial role as a powerful tool for growth. By intentionally using our conscious mind, we can influence and persuade our unconscious mind of its innate capabilities for intuitive tasks. Through focused thought, reflection, and practice, we create a bridge between the conscious intent and the unconscious mind's vast reservoir of intuitive knowledge. This not only encourages the growth of our intuitive skills but also strengthens the connection between the conscious and unconscious aspects of our minds, leading to a more harmonized and insightful experience of the intuitive world.

The Higher-Conscious Mind

In this section, we explore the concept of the higher conscious mind, a pivotal part of the cohesive system that makes up the three minds. While the book lays the groundwork for this understanding, it is important to note that specific techniques for harnessing the power of the higher-conscious mind are covered in depth in my live classes.

The higher-conscious mind is synonymous with what many refer to as the "higher self" or the "superconscious mind." It can be seen as the wise, guiding spirit within us, acting as our bridge to the higher realms of existence. Think of it as the divine or "God spirit" that resides within each of us. This aspect of our consciousness holds the potential to shape our reality to our desires, provided we engage in effective actions and processes to work harmoniously with it.

The higher-conscious mind respects the autonomy and free will of the conscious mind, interfering only when explicitly requested. It operates from a place of unconditional love and forgiveness, acknowledging the fundamental truth that we are all one.

We can intentionally connect with our higher self through the unconscious mind, with the conscious decision to do so acting as the catalyst. All three minds work as a cohesive system that is central to our health, vitality, and evolutionary growth. The conscious mind, with its capacity for reasoning, planning, and deliberate action, serves as the navigator, steering us toward our goals and desires. Parallel to this, the unconscious mind holds memories, instincts, and emotions, orchestrating life-sustaining processes without our active awareness. Additionally, it connects us to the higher-conscious mind or our higher self, which offers expansive guidance and wisdom from a more interconnected viewpoint.

This collaboration among the three minds creates a more powerful synergy, promoting healing, growth, and transformation. By achieving harmony among these aspects of our mind, we are better equipped to process experiences, make choices that resonate with our highest good, and tap into deeper levels of intuition and understanding.

Animals, on the other hand, possess a keenly developed unconscious mind, otherwise known as the "animal brain," and their conscious minds have much less influence, if any at all. This allows them to sense their environment deeply and collect raw and unfiltered energetic data. It also gives animals a direct pathway to psychic and intuitive skills, such as telepathy, without the inner distractions we face. They are true masters of energetic communication, offering unparalleled guidance for humans who are eager to enhance and develop their abilities.

The Five Senses

In our exploration of human perception and intuition, the five senses act as the primary pathways through which we engage with the world around us. These senses do more than just help us navigate our environment; they are intricately linked to how we intuitively collect information. In this section, we'll explore the unique ways we receive intuitive and telepathic information through these sensory pathways and connect them to what I call "your best clair"—your most attuned intuitive sense, such as clairvoyance (seeing) or clairaudience (hearing).

Our goal is to illuminate how these conventional senses can serve as powerful tools to understand and develop our intuitive abilities. Recognizing which of the five senses you rely on most in your daily life is the first step toward understanding and harnessing your intuitive abilities. This insight allows you to explore the "clairs" in a way that aligns with your natural inclinations, making the process of developing these skills feel more intuitive and less like learning something entirely new.

As you read through this content, I encourage you to pay attention to the senses that resonate with you the most—the ones you find yourself relying on frequently. You might discover one particular sense that makes you think, *This is exactly me!* Alternatively, you might find that a blend of several senses best describes your primary way of experiencing the world.

Visual Sense

The visual sense enables us not only to perceive the world in all its vivid detail but also to create moving or still images within our mind's eye. This ability allows us to visualize scenarios created by our imagination, recall memories in detail, and imagine new concepts with clarity. Whether it's envisioning a serene beach at sunset or picturing a bustling city street, visual people can explore worlds beyond their immediate surroundings, creating intricate visual narratives without opening their eyes.

The visual sense is linked to clairvoyance, a form of extrasensory perception that translates as "clear seeing." It involves receiving intuitive information visually, often as images (moving or still), colors, or visions that are thought of in the mind. Those with a heightened visual sense may find themselves naturally inclined to having clairvoyant abilities, experiencing vivid dreams and visual flashes of insight, or even seeing symbols during meditation.

Questions to Test if You're Visual

1. When you think of a recent place you've visited, can you create a picture of it in your mind, including colors and shapes?
2. When you read a book or story, can you easily imagine and visualize the scenes, characters, and settings described in the text?
3. Can you recall specific visual information, such as the layout of a room in a home you've visited recently?

In the world of animal communication, people with a strong visual sense often receive telepathic images that convey messages from animals. For example, a person might suddenly visualize a specific toy, which might indicate a dog's desire to play with it. You may also receive images showing preferred locations, such as a lake, and even memories from the animal's perspective.

Story Example

During a session with Molly, a charming dog, and her owner, Nichol, one particular question Nichol had was about Molly's favorite places. When I asked Molly this question, she instantly sent me a vivid mental image of a beautiful lake edged by a pathway and lush with foliage. This picture was clear in my mind, and upon sharing it with Nichol, her response revealed a touching connection; she recognized it as her family's favorite vacation spot, a place they retreated to every year and where they took Molly boating with them.

Auditory Sense

The auditory sense is our natural ability to perceive sound by detecting vibrations through our ears. However, this sense also encompasses the capacity to hear sounds, words, sentences, or even complex dialogues in our minds. For those of you who have a lot of internal "self-talk," you are likely well connected to your auditory sense. This internal auditory experience plays a key role in how we process thoughts, recall memories, and even motivate ourselves.

This sense is linked to clairaudience and allows people to receive information beyond the physical realm. Clairaudients process auditory psychic or telepathic information as intuitive insights that come in the form of voices, sounds, or music in the mind. Though it feels similar to self-talk, it is information coming in from external sources.

Questions to Test if You're Auditory

1. Pick someone close to you. Can you imagine what they would sound like if they talked to you in Mickey Mouse's voice?
2. Do you get songs stuck in your head and play them internally over and over?
3. Do you have strong self-talk or inner dialog?

In animal communication, clairaudient abilities might show up as intuitively picking up an animal's messages as words or sentences in the mind. You might "hear" them in your mind or even see the words in your head. The information may come through like a thought, and it might even have your own "voice," but it isn't actually coming from you. For example, a clairaudient person might hear in their mind a specific word or phrase to describe a favorite activity of the animal, like "play in the water." I often see this happen, where the animal will bring up something to me that they want, and the owner shares that they recently "had that same thought."

Story Example

I was conducting a session with a husband and wife and their mini horse, Tango. Tango excitedly shared with me through an auditory transmission: "I'd like Dad to take me on walks around the neighborhood!" I distinctly heard this sentence in my mind, and although it had the same familiar tone as my own internal self-talk, my experience as an animal communicator allowed me to differentiate between my thoughts and the messages originating from Tango. I shared this with the wife, and she chuckled, mentioning that her husband had "had that same thought recently." I laughed, knowing that the thought wasn't originally his but telepathic information he'd received from Tango.

Kinesthetic Sense

The kinesthetic sense involves navigating the world through physical sensations and emotions or having a "gut feeling." This sense allows people to feel others' emotions as if they were their own, providing a profound empathetic connection. It also encompasses receiving impressions or a deep sense of "knowing" something without a logical basis for this knowledge.

When linked to clairsentience (clear feeling) and claircognizance (clear knowing), the kinesthetic sense transcends conventional boundaries, enabling a person to perceive psychic information through extended feeling, physical sensations, and that sense of "knowing." Clairsentients experience a heightened form of this sense, where they might feel a sudden discomfort in the knee around someone who is recovering from a knee injury. Additionally, those with claircognizance may also be introduced to new information about a friend's romantic fling and suddenly receive the impression that "they won't work out." You don't know how you know, but you do, and it ends up coming true.

Questions to Test if You're Kinesthetic

1. Have you ever walked into a room and immediately felt its energy, including people's emotions?
2. Do you often "just know" things about people or situations without knowing why or how?
3. Can you sense the history or energy of an object by touching it or being near it?
4. Can you "replay" a memory in your mind of something that happened in your past? When you do recall the memory, can you do so without needing to remember the words or images associated with it, or do you simply remember it because you know it happened?

Kayla, my associate trainer and a master communicator at Pet Talk Communications, is highly kinesthetic in how she receives information. People who are more kinesthetic often find it harder to recognize this trait in themselves. Kayla explains it to our students like this: When she first connects with an animal, it feels as if the animal's presence is in her space, and she can sense their energy. When she begins a conversation, she doesn't hear words; rather, it feels like she's recalling a conversation she had the day before. The story example below shows how this works.

Story Example

I once called Kayla to talk to my dog, Ginger, because Ginger seemed to have something going on with her throat, and I was too worried to gather clear information myself. We were waiting for test results from the vet, and I wanted to hear from Ginger's perspective how she was doing.

When Kayla connected with Ginger, she first felt her nurturing and happy "mama bear" energy. During the conversation, when she asked Ginger questions, she described the experience as similar to replaying a conversation in her head that she'd already had.

In describing the experience, Kayla said, "Have you ever replayed a memory of a conversation you had with someone? You think about it, replay it in your mind, and wish you had said 'this' instead of 'that.' That is what it is like for me when communicating with an animal. I'm not hearing the words, but it's as if I am replaying the memory of the conversation just like I was there."

When she asked Ginger specifically how she was feeling, she told me that Ginger replied, "I'm fine, I'm fine," seeming very happy and that her throat was okay. Kayla didn't necessarily receive this in words; it was more like she was there with Ginger, knew this conversation had happened, and could recall it like a memory to share it with me. This describes her kinesthetic sense coming through as her way of "knowing" or receiving impressions. Also, Ginger did turn out to be just fine!

Additionally, someone might receive feelings in the body that are an expression of the messages coming through. For example, I was doing a session with a horse once, and all of a sudden, I felt a pain in my teeth on the right side of my mouth. Physical sensations do not *always* come from the animals, so it is important not to assume but to clarify with them if the information is accurate. I asked the horse if she was experiencing pain in her mouth. She said yes, and that was why she was behaving abnormally while being ridden with the bit in her mouth. Her owner took her to the vet following her appointment, and it turned out to be true. They treated her, and she was soon back to normal!

Clairalience and Clairgustance

Our understanding of and connection to the world around us goes beyond just what we can see, hear, and touch. Less common yet equally meaningful are the insights we gain through our senses of smell and taste, known as clairalience (clear smelling) and clairgustance (clear tasting). You might think of these two senses as fun additions to your primary sense(s) that come into play just when you need them.

Story Example: Clairalience

I conducted a session with a cat named Rico, who wanted to voice his opinion on home fragrances. During the session, an unexpected yet potent floral aroma enveloped me. It was clear as day, yet not a part of my physical environment. Rico then conveyed his distaste for the aromatic assault of wall plug-ins! He shared how their intense fragrances overwhelmed his delicate feline senses. The owners completely understood and immediately removed the plug-ins.

Story Example: Clairgustance

While in a session with two delightful dogs, I asked one of them to share with me his favorite things. A vivid taste of french fries suddenly overcame me, which, of course, I wasn't mad about, but I hadn't eaten any french fries. The taste revelation was as surprising to me as it was to the owner, who revealed that just before our session, a drive-through snack had indeed included some fries for the furry companions. The dog was cleverly communicating his enjoyment of this snack as one of his favorite things.

As we bring this chapter to a gentle close, I invite you to pause and reflect on the sensory pathways that resonate most deeply with you. It's an opportunity to explore all of your perceptions and to note which of the senses speaks to you with the greatest clarity. Keep a journal to record your observations, allowing you to explore your sensory experiences with thoughtful introspection. Doing so will not only help you deepen your understanding of your own natural preferences but also serve as a foundation upon which we will build throughout the rest of this book.

Together, we will venture further into the power of our intuitive senses, unearthing new insights and expanding the boundaries of our spiritual awareness.

What We Learned in Chapter 1:

- The profound impact of energy on our surroundings through vibrational frequencies, as evidenced by Dr. Masaru Emoto's research on water crystals, showcasing the interconnectedness between human emotional energy and physical matter, with implications for telepathic communication and understanding nonverbal psychic animal communication.

- Understanding the intricate workings of the mind through the three key components—the unconscious, conscious, and higher-conscious minds—provides a cheat code for deciphering incoming telepathic and energetic information, explaining how sensory data is processed and filtered to shape our internal reality, behaviors, and ultimately, our external experiences.

- The five senses are vital pathways through which we engage with the world, not only aiding in navigating our environment but also playing a key role in how we gather intuitive information. Understanding and leveraging our dominant sense can enhance our intuitive abilities more quickly, guiding us to explore and develop our natural inclinations for intuitive senses like clairvoyance or clairaudience. Identifying your primary sense preference is the initial step towards honing your intuitive skills, making the process feel more aligned with your inherent strengths.

CHAPTER 2

Unveiling Telepathic Connection

First, let's demystify "telepathy" by stripping away the Hollywood glamor and looking at it as a practical way to exchange information energetically. This isn't about mind-reading but how thoughts, images, and feelings can move from one mind to another. It's something we've all experienced! For instance, have you ever craved a specific type of food, only for your friend to suggest going out to eat exactly that? This isn't just coincidence; it's an energetic transfer of ideas between you two, where one picks up on the telepathic thought of the other as it pertains to a shared goal and activity.

This kind of telepathic communication is a natural form of interaction that everyone is born with, and it happens more often than we realize. As I mentioned in Chapter 1, this capability operates largely in the background, managed by our unconscious minds without our active awareness.

Consider another common scenario: thinking of someone right before they call you. The thought of them pops into your head, and the next thing you know, your phone is ringing, and it's them on the other line. You may answer and say, "How funny! I was just thinking about you!" Your thought about the person created an energetic link between your minds, prompting them to reach out. Alternatively, you could have picked up the energetic alert that you were on their mind before they called you.

These are common occurrences in our everyday lives. However, some individuals, particularly those who work with animal communication, have honed in on this innate ability to intentionally engage in telepathic connections. It is not a matter of if we can; it's a matter of how. The question then becomes, how can we more consciously develop and apply this skill in our interactions with the natural world and, more specifically, with our animal friends?

To understand this better, we need to explore the concept of "thought forms." These are simple yet potent pockets of information that exist in our minds and can be energetically transmitted to others. For telepathy to occur, these thought forms need to be energized; without energy, they remain inactive. An illustrative example is my brother's childhood attempt to move a pen with his mind. I watched as he gazed intensely at it from across the room. His eyes were fixed on the pen, his eyebrows scrunched with concentration, and his fingers pressed against his temples as he concentrated on moving the pen with sheer willpower. Despite his intense and adorable concentration, he missed a crucial element: the action of directing energy to make the pen move.

In our three-dimensional reality, we know that intentional action is required to move the pen, such as walking over and moving it with our hand. Even so, this story serves as a perfect metaphor to explain how thought forms and telepathy work. For telepathic communication to be effective, it requires not just focus and intention but directed energy. This energy acts as the fuel, propelling the thought from our minds to the intended recipient.

Imagine thought forms as grapes clustered on a vine. A simple idea might fit neatly into a single grape or thought form, while more complex ideas will spread out across multiple grapes in a cluster. For example, if I decide to bring one of my horses apples today and want to convey this through telepathy, my unconscious mind would focus the image or idea of one apple into a single thought form. I would then give my unconscious mind direction to energetically send this single "grape" of thought from my mind to his.

In other words, a straightforward or single idea, such as the apple, is like one grape: easy to conceptualize and send. In contrast, a complex idea spans several grapes or thought forms, all connected on the same vine but containing different facets of the broader concept. These clusters allow for a more nuanced message, transmitting a series of related thoughts or images simultaneously.

By thinking of thought forms this way, it becomes easier to grasp how we can package and send both simple and complex ideas telepathically. Whether sending the notion of a single apple or a more intricate message, the process involves selecting (or creating) the appropriate "grape" or cluster of grapes, energizing it, and sending it to the receiver.

This concept sheds light on why the information received telepathically can sometimes seem vague or abstract, as I mentioned before, like getting ingredients to a recipe without being told what the recipe is. This is particularly relevant when trying to communicate with animals. For instance, it's not as simple as your dog Fido conveying a detailed account of his activities on a specific morning, including the outfits of his owners, what was on television that day, or the exact layout of the home.

Likewise, this complexity extends to the challenge of receiving names during a psychic session. Names, created by humans and involving specific sequences of vowels, consonants, and spelling, are tough to encapsulate and transmit as thought forms. This difficulty arises because thought forms are more naturally suited to conveying images, emotions, or general words rather than a precise, constructed language construct like a name.

Despite the complexity of linguistic information, communicators who are predominantly auditory and can "hear" or "see" words telepathically can still receive a substantial portion. This is due to two factors. First, the animals themselves recognize these words with the corresponding feelings or images, effectively sending them through thought forms. Second, the communicator's unconscious mind plays a crucial role in translating this information into auditory form, be it a single word or an entire sentence.

Names (due to their specificity and the exact sequence of letters they require) pose a greater challenge for this type of communication. In contrast, conveying a desire like "I want to go in the backyard" is more straightforward in the psychic space. Such messages are easier for the animal to encode in a thought form and simpler for the communicator's unconscious mind to interpret.

Even though accurately receiving a name is rare, it's not entirely out of the realm of possibility. I remember a session early in my career with a couple and their dog that really drove this point home. The husband, skeptical from the start, challenged me by saying to the wife prior to the session, "If she can figure out the nickname I call the dog, I'll believe her."

When they asked me to ask the dog for his nickname, I felt my nerves kick in. Aware of the difficulties associated with the names, yet unclear on the specificities, I proceeded with caution. I focused, hoping to connect and receive a clear answer. The response came quickly—"Bud, Buddy!"—but its simplicity made me second-guess its validity.

Doubting myself, I continued probing, sensing a theme of brotherhood or camaraderie linked to the nickname. Still unsure, I unconsciously referred to the dog as "Buddy" in the conversation. That's when the wife excitedly confirmed that "Buddy" was, indeed, the special nickname used by the husband and their son for each other and the dog. It highlighted a shared bond within the family.

I immediately wished I had trusted the initial, simple message that had come through. This experience taught me an invaluable lesson about trusting the process and the importance of voicing even those messages that seem too straightforward. Names might be notoriously tricky in telepathic communication, but this instance proved that accuracy isn't impossible—it's about having faith in the information as it's received.

Our exploration into telepathy reveals it to be an innate, though frequently overlooked, human skill. This capability is not something we need to learn from scratch; rather, it's a skill our unconscious mind is already equipped to handle and, as you can see now, is already doing to some degree. To telepathically transmit images, concepts, or complex ideas, the process does not require us to laboriously encode each message into numerous thought forms. Instead, the unconscious mind intuitively manages this process on our behalf. However, grasping the underlying mechanics is important in understanding how to do it, just as you'd learn the basic operations of a car before driving it.

Critical to the successful transmission of thought forms is the presence of "energy in motion." This dynamic force is propelled by life-force energy—a ubiquitous, intangible power that permeates our existence. In my classes, we use life-force energy to generate "mana," a word of Polynesian origin that refers to supernatural or divine power. It is also known by various names across cultures, such as chi, prana, orgone energy, and od. This is the energy we draw into our lungs with each breath and the vibrant aura we often feel in rooms brimming with excitement. The mere act of entering such a space can elevate our mood, often without us being aware of the origin of this collective energy.

You just feel that energy and it's almost infectious. Similarly, hearing a baby laugh has a unique way of drawing you into its joy. Simply by being present in that space and absorbing the vibrational frequency of the laughter, you may find yourself laughing along, swept up in the infectious cheer.

Life-force energy is omnipresent and infinitely abundant. It cannot be created or destroyed, but it can be transferred, shared, diminished, or amplified at any given moment. This shows us the potential within us to harness and use this energy consciously, not only for telepathic communication but also as a means to positively influence and interact with the world around us.

To harness life-force energy for telepathic communication, it's essential to recognize that energy, a resource we're always connected to, can be deliberately engaged and directed through specific actions. This process can help the movement of thought forms from sender to receiver.

The creation of energy within the body is similar to initiating a physical response that signals the unconscious mind. The unconscious mind is particularly receptive when it perceives physical proof or action as part of learning or doing something new. In other words, a physical stimulus can convince the unconscious mind that "We're doing this, and I mean business." Thus, by introducing a physical stimulus at the onset of your practice, you can effectively prompt your unconscious mind to augment the influx of life-force energy within your body. This energy then serves as the "fuel" for sending telepathic thoughts to their intended destination.

The equation here is simple: Energy combined with action creates results. By engaging both the conscious and unconscious minds, along with a physical stimulus, we prime the body for the successful creation and dispatch of thought forms. Incorporating physical activities, such as jumping, rubbing your hands together, or even shuffling your feet, acts as a directive to the unconscious mind, signaling the intent to create an excess amount of life force energy with determination.

This preparation involves the conscious mind selecting a physical activity that will serve as the stimulus for connecting telepathically with an animal. Along with physical movement, integrating breathwork enhances this energy-building process. A particular technique we teach is "ha" breathing, characterized by a pronounced inhalation through the nose followed by a forceful, slow, and auditory exhale through the mouth, much like when we were kids and would breathe our hot breath onto the car window so we could draw on it.

By combining physical stimuli with "ha" breathing, we not only generate but accumulate life-force energy in the body. This prepares us to channel and project telepathic thoughts more efficiently. Now, are you ready to practice?

Building Life Force Energy Through "Ha" Breathing

1. Pick a physical activity to serve as your physical stimulus for the exercise. Opt for something that gets your body moving yet allows you

to remain in your comfort zone. In a live class, we prefer rubbing our hands together vigorously, as it's a simple motion that can be performed while seated, but you can also incorporate other movements, such as jumping or stretching.

2. Mentally or verbally send a command to your unconscious mind: *Unconscious mind, we are building a surplus of life-force energy in the body now, and I mean business about it.*

3. Begin your physical stimulus and "ha" breathing technique. Breathe in through your nose for four to five seconds, filling up the lungs and rib cage. Then, exhale with a pronounced and slow "ha" sound through your mouth. If you wish, you may practice beforehand and place your hand in front of your mouth to feel the warmth of your breath. That warmth is evidence of correct execution.

4. Pair your physical stimulus with "ha" breathing for four complete breaths (in through the nose and out through the mouth is one complete breath). Visualize drawing energy into your body with each breath in, and imagine storing and preserving this energy within you with each exhale.

5. After completing four breaths, discontinue your physical stimulus but maintain the "ha" breathing.

6. Continue to draw energy inward on the inhale and focus on conserving it internally on the exhale. Imagine this energy filling every part of your being, from the soles of your feet to the crown of your head.

7. Once you feel completely full of energy, relax and allow your breath to go back to its natural rhythm. Take a moment to observe any new sensations or changes within your body, acknowledging the presence and distribution of the energy you've cultivated.

Should you begin to feel lightheaded at any moment during your practice, it's important to pause and allow your breath to return to its natural pace. This sensation is a direct result of introducing a higher volume of energy and oxygen to your system, particularly to your brain. With consistent practice, you'll gradually build up stamina for this heightened state.

It's also common to experience changes in body temperature as your energy levels increase, causing you to feel warmer. Remember, though, if at any given time the sensations become unpleasant or uncomfortable, give yourself permission to take a break.

Various methods exist to strengthen telepathic connections. One particularly effective technique involves enhancing your peripheral vision, also known as "The Learning State." This practice is geared toward decelerating brainwave activity, creating an optimal state for learning, entering a trance, and honing intuitive abilities.

"The Learning State" refers to the meditative act of fixed gazing, which gradually extends to a widened field of vision. The method not only calms the mind but opens it up to deeper levels of awareness and connectivity. By slowing down the brainwaves and generating a light trance state (which is nothing other than focused relaxation), the conscious mind takes a backseat, allowing the unconscious mind a clearer pathway to receiving psychic information.

"The Learning State"

1. Pick a spot on the wall just above eye level to look at, positioned so you're not tilting your head uncomfortably upwards but rather where your vision gently gazes just beneath your eyebrows.

2. Keep your eyes fixed on that spot and allow your mind to relax or go "loose."

3. Within a few moments, you will notice your vision begin to "spread out" as you begin to have more of an awareness of your peripheral vision.

4. Continue to focus on the chosen spot. Then, gradually shift your attention to your peripheral vision, allowing it to become more dominant while still looking at that spot. A useful tip is to place your hands near the sides of your face with fingers wiggling and then

slowly move them outwards. Keep your eyes on the spot, but be aware of how your peripheral vision stretches to follow your hands until they're just barely out of sight. Drop and relax your hands.

5. Stay in this state and breathe for a few minutes or as long as you can.

The Learning State not only helps you get ready to perform intuitive tasks but also any activity where easy information retention is desired, like reading a book (*cough* this one *cough*), studying, or attending a class.

Another simple technique to prepare for intuitive work is navel breathing. Begin by focusing your awareness on the crown of your head. As you inhale, visualize drawing energy in through the crown. When you exhale, shift your focus to your belly button. Repeat this process for at least one minute. You may do this practice with your eyes closed or open.

Maintain a Practice Log

Keeping a practice log is immensely valuable as it serves as an excellent guide for effectively developing your skills. Whether you're undertaking simple meditation or any form of intuitive work, it's useful to pay attention to which senses feel most engaged, especially as the more you practice, the more the answers can change! Ask yourself, during your meditation or intuitive practice, did you easily visualize images, feel physical sensations, have a clear knowing about certain topics, or find yourself having an internal dialogue? Write down your experience and go back to the senses in Chapter 1 to log which ones were prominent and "online" during that practice. Noting these experiences can help you identify which senses are more active so you can focus on strengthening them for more efficient skill development.

Furthermore, tracking the symbols that appear during your practice can enhance your intuitive abilities. Symbols might manifest as recurring images, shapes, colors, animals, or even food items, and they often hold personal significance to your unconscious mind—so please refrain from using Google! A symbol's meaning will be different for you than for someone else. Writing down these symbols and interpreting what they mean to *you* can significantly aid in translating telepathic information later on. For example, a rose to one person might signify love and comfort, whereas a rose to someone else might signify heartbreak and sadness. When a recurring symbol pops into your awareness, write it down and ask yourself, *What does _____ mean to me?* The immediate answers that come to mind, whether they are love, acceptance, or perhaps loss and sadness, provide crucial insights that reflect your unique interpretations.

When it comes to documenting intuitive practice, approaches vary. Some find that writing down their experiences as they occur helps slow down their brainwaves, fostering a smoother flow of unconscious information onto paper. This method could deepen your connection with your intuition by capturing thoughts, symbols, and sensations as they arise.

Alternatively, if writing distracts you during practice, consider voice recording your results. Using your phone or another device, record any symbols, words, images, emotions, or feelings that surface. Speaking out loud without filtering or analyzing allows you to gather raw, unedited insights. Later, these recordings can be revisited to collect tangible information, particularly beneficial for practices like animal communication.

Whether you choose to write or record, the key is to document your intuitive processes in a way that suits you best. This will enable a more profound exploration and understanding of your psychic abilities. Anytime my students ask if they should do one thing over another, I respond that they should do the thing that gets them the best results!

What We Learned in Chapter 2:

- Telepathy is an energetic exchange of thoughts, images, and feelings, commonly experienced in daily life (e.g., thinking of someone before they call), and can be consciously developed for intentional communication with animals by directing energy to transmit thought forms.

- Communicators can receive words telepathically because animals send thought forms with associated feelings or images, and the communicator's unconscious mind translates them into auditory form, though specific names are more challenging to convey.
- Life-force energy is abundant and can be consciously harnessed and directed through physical actions and breathwork to facilitate telepathic communication, as energy combined with action creates results.
- "Ha" breathing techniques to generate life-force energy and use it for telepathic communication.
- "The Learning State" technique for inducing a natural state of trance and relaxation to enhance focus in animal communication.
- Keeping a practice log helps develop intuitive skills by tracking engaged senses and recurring symbols during meditation or intuitive work, allowing for focused skill strengthening and personal symbol interpretation. Documenting experiences through writing or voice recording can deepen your connection with your intuition, providing valuable insights for practices like telepathic communication.

CHAPTER 3

Introduction to Animal Communication

Animal communication is a fascinating and deeply intuitive field that bridges the gap between humans and animals, allowing for a profound understanding and connection that transcends the spoken word. This practice, often referred to as interspecies communication, involves telepathically sending and receiving messages, emotions, and sensations directly from one mind to another, regardless of species.

At its core, animal communication is built on the foundation of empathy, respect, and an open heart. It enables us to listen to animals in a much more profound way, tapping into an instinctual and spiritual dialogue that we are all born with but have forgotten due to the modern world's distractions, social "norms," and more.

Animals communicate telepathically in three ways: through *pictures, words,* and *feelings.* Our minds are continuously processing information more than we're consciously aware of. We do not realize how much of this information we are telepathically projecting, which is why my animal clients often say that their owners are already doing it but need to practice!

Animals can also engage in this constant exchange of information, though they have a greater ability to control it, choosing when to "switch on" or "switch off" their telepathic abilities. They can do so without any conscious thought, as this type of communication comes so naturally to them.

Consider a flock of birds perched together on a rooftop. Suddenly, as though following an invisible signal, they all take flight, moving in unison to another location. While part of this behavior can be attributed to biological instincts, I would argue that biological instincts are directly connected and related to their telepathic abilities, as there is an undeniable element of shared energetic connection. In these moments, the birds are "switched on," connected by a collective consciousness that guides their actions harmoniously.

On the flip side, a predator hunting its prey benefits from being "switched off" telepathically to avoid alerting its target. The element of surprise is crucial for a successful hunt, making it counterproductive for a predator to broadcast its intentions telepathically to its prey. This nuanced control over their communicative abilities highlights the complex and fascinating ways in which animals interact with each other and their environment.

For a telepathic exchange of information to occur between two minds, there must be some level of consent; otherwise, the message might not be received properly. This principle applies equally to animals and humans. Often, humans give this consent unconsciously, especially with their pets, due to the strong bond and rapport that exist in their relationship. It is within this space that unintentional communication frequently happens. For instance, while you're engaged in household chores, you might suddenly think about feeding your cat or walking your dog. Sometimes, these seemingly random thoughts can actually be messages from your pets, mistakenly perceived as your internal reminders of their needs.

When animals engage in telepathic communication with pictures, words, and feelings, they can transmit these elements sequentially or simultaneously. Animals are pros at telepathy, and to them, this is the most efficient way to communicate. It's important to remember that how you perceive these telepathic messages—whether as pictures, words, or feelings—depends on your neurological makeup and how it processes sensory information, as discussed in Chapter 1.

Your primary "clair(s)" is not a magical sixth sense; it's simply an extension of your everyday senses. For visual individuals, images may be received vividly and easily. Those with a strong kinesthetic sense may experience clear feelings or intuitive "impressions" that provide insight into a situation. Meanwhile, auditory people might find it easier to hear words or see sentences unfold in their mind's eye.

Our ability and readiness to hear and collect information stems from our openness and capacity for receiving—and this isn't limited to just telepathic messages. Throughout my career, I've discovered how deeply this work has mirrored insights about myself and the ways I engage with the world around me. The way I present myself in my personal life projects directly into my interactions within the animal realm. If I am guarded and hesitant to accept love and connection in my human relationships, this disposition reflects in my receptiveness in other areas of life as well.

However, the moment I began acknowledging this pattern and consciously chose to remain as open as I could, I noticed a significant improvement in my ability to communicate with animals. Still, I am human, and I work on opening more and more to life every day. This transformation extends beyond interpersonal relationships; it encompasses all aspects of life. It's about taking intentional deep breaths, appreciating your surroundings, living in the moment, and cherishing the small joys. By opening your heart to love, to the wonder of existence, and allowing life to crack you open in the most beautiful ways, you'll observe remarkable enhancements in your intuitive capacities to receive messages. After all, everything in this universe is connected.

Receiving Incoming Information

Anyone can learn to be an animal communicator, but the way to become skilled is to learn to properly interpret the information. A dog might send a picture of their favorite toy, and it may not be as clear as seeing a fox toy with a torn right ear and only three legs and a tail. We may get a brief mental image of the outline of the toy and maybe an impression of the kind of animal that it is or hear the word "fox." Or, heaven forbid, I've had my fair share of dogs who have tons of toys, and they show me a giant pile and say, "These!"

The messages can sometimes be a little abstract, and I always tell my students that part of the job is becoming a really good detective and translator so we can provide the most accurate information. This does come with practice, but ultimately, it also comes with an acute sense of self-awareness, which we will explore in the following chapters.

I'm often asked whether the dialogue from animals sounds like a different voice. For me, the answer is no, but I do hear different pitches and tempos. This can make it tricky, especially for beginners, to tell the difference between their thoughts and incoming messages. Many of my students initially joke that they feel like they're talking to themselves. This is completely normal! Remember, you've been naturally communicating this way your whole life without realizing it. Now, you're trying to do it consciously, so it might feel a bit awkward at first.

The more you practice, the more skilled you'll become at differentiating your thoughts from incoming external information. It's just like riding a bike: You're engaging new muscles for a new activity, and with practice, these actions become muscle memory, making you better at it over time.

My earliest advice to students is to let go of the expectation of getting things "right" during their initial practices. If you're in a safe setting where there's no pressure to be accurate, it's perfectly okay to get things wrong. This allows you to be clear without any attachment to a particular outcome. Just play along, let the process flow, and observe what your body is doing without worrying about gathering correct information. Later in the book, I will share with you a full "how to" to begin your connection practices. For now, let's continue to build a rock-solid foundation.

When an animal communicator asks questions during a session, they can do so either silently in their mind or out loud to the animal. There's no right or wrong way to do it. In my sessions, I often use both methods. Asking questions in the mind is much faster because sending a telepathic thought form takes less time than mentally processing and then verbally communicating.

When I ask questions out loud, it is to keep the client informed and prevent interruptions while I'm getting answers from the animal. Then, I share the information aloud as it comes through. Sharing information as it comes helps me clear my mind, making it easier for more details to come through smoothly. It also allows messages to flow through my unconscious mind before my conscious mind has a chance to filter or question them.

If an animal communicator is not conducting a session live, they might write the messages down as they come through or voice record them as they come to mind. This serves the same purpose of capturing the information before the conscious mind has a chance to interfere. However, that doesn't necessarily mean that the information is going to be 100% accurate because, remember, our unconscious minds have their own filters. We still must stay humble and on our toes in navigating the information to the best of our ability. Some communications might be clear and to the point, while others might require more clarification to ensure we collect the most accurate information.

An Example of an Easy Dialogue

One afternoon, I was taking a walk with my beloved dog, Jo. Since we lived in a townhouse without a fenced yard, we often went on walks so he could get fresh air and sunshine and go to the bathroom. That afternoon, I noticed that he was refusing to walk on the grass. I asked him out loud, "Jo, why won't you go on the grass to go potty?"

In my mind, I heard a response like my own self-talk, but I'm experienced enough to recognize the difference when it isn't mine: "Because the grass was just cut and I'm white." At the same time, he showed me an image of his fluffy white paws and legs. I replied in my mind, *Yeah, so?*

He answered, "I don't want the grass to make my fur green!"

Puzzled, I said, "Why would that make your fur green?" thinking this had never happened before. Where had he picked up such an idea? He then

41

showed me an image of my white sneakers with green-stained soles from when I'd cut my mom's grass nearly a year ago. I had completely forgotten about that and burst out laughing. I quickly assured him that his fur wouldn't turn green because the grass here had been cut a while ago but that I understood his concern.

Breaking this down, Jo had seen my stained sneakers from when I'd cut the grass and thought the same would happen to his own white fur. You might be thinking, *But dogs don't see the same colors that we do, so how did he know to call it "white" or "green?"* There are two possibilities here that could be true in a conversation such as this one. First of all, I always tell Jo that the white parts of his fur look sparkly in the sun, so he knows he is "white." If an animal shares color labels in a session, they could have picked up the color label from their environment by watching and listening to people, matching the label we give it to whichever color or shade they see. The second possibility is that when they present a color or shade (or multiple), our unconscious minds will translate that information in a way that we already perceive it, giving it the color label we know and understand it to be.

An Example of a Conversation That May Need More Clarification

I was conducting a session with a client named Georgia and her dog, Iris. Toward the end, we asked Iris if she had any wants, needs, or requests. She replied in words, saying, "I want to do flips!" Not fully understanding her response and knowing from experience that words communicated by animals don't always directly translate properly to human activities, I asked out loud for clarification, "What does that mean to you?" She replied with a picture of her in Georgia's arms, being held up high (not "flipping" as we would think of it).

Still confused, I prodded for more clarification and said playfully out loud, "That is definitely not a flip, though! Do you just want to be up high?" Iris responded this time in words, repeating, "In the air! In the air!" I laughed, and before I could share this part aloud, Georgia chimed in that she would sometimes pick her up and toss her gently onto the bed from a distance. I asked Iris if that was what she was trying to show me, as I was only receiving a still image of her being held up and out, accompanied by the words "In the air! In the air!" It wasn't quite giving me the full picture yet because Iris was so excited she hadn't followed up with any information about the actual toss onto the bed.

To clarify if we were all on the same page, I asked the question aloud and sent Iris a moving picture of what it might look like for her to be lifted and tossed onto the bed from a distance. Iris excitedly said, "Yes! That's it!" Georgia said that she would do that and assumed that Iris liked it because, when she'd get close to the bed, Iris would try to kick off Georgia's chest and initiate the launch. Georgia had started feeling for Iris's anticipated self-launch and then would toss her, hoping that was what she wanted! However, she wasn't sure if that was what Iris was asking for until she brought it up herself in our session.

When I ask questions out loud, the animal does not receive the question aurally. They don't need to be in earshot of my voice. Asking the question out loud is simply for the client. As I create the intention to send the question to the animal, my unconscious mind, at rapid speed, creates and sends the telepathic thought form that can reach the animal before I finish saying the question out loud. Telepathy is a much faster way of giving and receiving information.

Animals can respond in many different ways. Some are quick-witted and send me detailed information rapidly, while others, who perhaps prefer a slower and simpler life, may share minimal information at a more relaxed pace. Although this isn't always the case because opposites do attract, I often find that the human owner and their animal have matching communication styles, displaying their vibrational match in personality and energy. For example, an excited owner with many questions usually has an animal that provides lots of enthusiastic answers. On the other hand, human clients who are more conservative in conversation, tone, and energy often have animals that give simpler, more direct answers with fewer details. The fun part? You never really know what to expect with any session until you get in there!

When information isn't as clear, such as how Jo communicated about the grass, animal communicators shouldn't hesitate to ask follow-up questions for clarification. For example, in Georgia and Iris's case, if Georgia hadn't mentioned the toss, I would have continued to ask Iris more questions to understand what she wanted. If Iris couldn't provide clarity, I would then turn to Georgia to share what I'd gathered and ask if it meant anything to her. Fortunately, Georgia was a wonderful and willing participant. She shared the activity, which saved us time. This allowed us to make sure everyone was on the same page so we could move on to another topic.

Animal communication offers a wide range of benefits for both animals and their humans. It can help address behavioral issues, ease family transitions, provide insight into medical problems, and much more. By understanding an animal's thoughts and feelings, we can work to identify the root causes of behavioral problems, making it easier to find effective solutions. During family transitions, such as moving to a new home or welcoming a new pet, animal communication can reduce stress and anxiety by preparing the animal for changes. Additionally, it can offer valuable insights into medical issues that might not be immediately obvious, guiding veterinary care or helping the animal understand the importance of medical attention and treatment.

An animal communication session can dramatically improve the relationship between an animal and their people. By fostering better understanding and empathy, these sessions can strengthen bonds, enhance mutual trust, and create a more harmonious living environment. Overall, the benefits of animal communication extend far beyond addressing immediate concerns, contributing to the long-term well-being and happiness of both animals and their human companions.

However, while such communication can be incredibly powerful, it does have its limitations. Sometimes, issues in the home environment can be dealt with and fixed like magic, but it's important to remember that the solution is not always a quick fix. Both simple and complex issues can be addressed in a session, but the success of the outcome depends on various factors.

A simple case may only require ironing out the root cause of an issue, allowing the animal to "air their grievances," so to speak, and come up with a solution in one easy session. For example, Krista and Joey are clients of mine who do regular check-ins with their cats and dog. They have a particular sassy cat named Bitty, who once began a session with me by describing herself as "I am sweet and spicy." We can always rely on Bitty to bring an issue to the session and see immediate improvements once it's resolved. She may be spicy, but she's always reasonable!

In a recent session, Bitty expressed frustration with one of the other cats, Sophie. She complained that Sohpie tries to tell her what to do sometimes, and that Sophie was "making waves in the cat herd" trying to take one of the cats from her. Knowing the cat group well, I remembered Sophie's usual diplomacy among the cats and suspected that Bitty's issues stemmed from her own internal struggles. When I asked what was really going on, suggesting it wasn't truly about Sophie, Bitty admitted she felt pent up due to the full moon (animals can be very sensitive to this energy) and a spell of bad weather, which made her feel cooped up. Unable to figure out how to release her energy, she unfairly projected her frustration onto Sophie.

Realizing this, I redirected the conversation to address the root cause and find a solution. Bitty and I devised a plan for her to expend her energy by running around the house and on the cat shelves, and later outside in her favorite spots once the weather improved. This simple conversation allowed Bitty to safely express her frustration, uncover the true source, and create solutions, leading to immediate results.

After our call, Krista reported that Bitty showed immediate improvement as she chose to sit next to Sophie, acting kind and sweet.

While some cases, like Bitty's, are resolved quickly by uncovering the root cause and agreeing to solutions, others are more complex and require additional effort. Other factors that become relevant in more challenging cases are:

- **Unrealistic Owner Expectations:** This often relates to an animal's behavior. Many owners expect an animal communicator to simply tell their pet to stop an undesired behavior, but it's usually not that simple and can be unfair to the animal. For example, if a husky owner wants their dog to stop "tearing up the apartment," I am likely to hear from the husky that they have too much pent-up energy, lack of training, and/or no boundaries. The real solution is not to simply ask them to stop; rather, it involves the owner becoming educated about the breed and all of us creating a plan to meet the husky's needs. Achieving harmony at home then requires the owner to follow through on necessary steps, not just ask the animal to change.

- **Requiring Professional Training:** This often stems from unrealistic owner expectations. When a behavior issue arises, it usually reflects the human-animal relationship. While an animal communicator can powerfully facilitate an open discussion, helping the owner understand specifically what the animal needs from their perspective and what they're interested in, it's crucial for both to seek a professional trainer to establish healthy habits, boundaries, and harmony at home. An animal communicator ensures everyone is on board with the plan, but like telling your therapist you need to improve your fitness, while they can help discuss motivations, they aren't qualified to design a workout routine. Hiring a trainer provides the expertise needed for real-time implementation of the plan, benefiting both the owner and the pet. In my world, we call this "The Dream Team," which I will expand on later in this chapter.

- **Medical Root Causes:** Sometimes new behaviors, like aggression or a persistent limp, may have medical origins. Animal communicators (unless they're licensed veterinarians) and animals themselves cannot diagnose these issues. Animals can describe how they feel, but this should be seen as a clue for further investigation, not definitive evidence. Any expressed pain or discomfort from an animal during a session should always be followed up with a visit to a medical professional.

- **Animals with Cognitive Issues:** Cognitive decline or impairment can limit the effectiveness of a session. As animals age, they may naturally experience cognitive decline, similar to humans. Cognitive impairment can also result from mind-altering medications or sedation, including some pain medications, depending on the dosage. If an animal isn't cognitively available, an animal communicator may struggle to connect and communicate effectively. For example, I once conducted a session for Julie and her horse, Jax. She wanted to get his perspective on some medical issues they'd been trying to work through. When I tuned in, he seemed to connect with me for only moments at a time before I'd lose him. When he did connect, he would begin a sentence but then trail off and he'd be gone! This was abnormal, and as I mentioned it to the owner, she said, "Oh! The vet sedated him pretty heavily a few hours ago. He is coming off the sedation still, could that be it?" I giggled—that was definitely the issue! We rescheduled for the next day when he was sober again, and the connection went on as normal.

Sessions for Behavioral Issues

Dealing with behavioral problems is one of the most common topics when clients reach out to me. Issues include dogs barking too much, animals not getting along, cats favoring one owner over another, and pets urinating in inappropriate places!

As mentioned earlier, an owner might ask, "Can you ask them to stop doing that?" While I can certainly ask, depending on the issue at hand, this approach doesn't always address the underlying issue, so the behavior might not change. Key factors for successfully addressing behavioral issues include the owner's practical expectations (e.g., the husky example), breed and genetic suitability, the owner's willingness to put in the necessary effort, and the animal's readiness to make changes. Often, these behaviors are deep-rooted habits. Simply asking an animal to stop would be like telling someone to break a long-standing habit without offering any support for creating a healthier one. Animals also have independent minds; just because we ask them not to do something, it doesn't mean they're going to listen. Lastly, it also depends on if the animal sees the issue as an issue!

A Difference in Perspective: Lucy, the Dog Who Loved People

I was once at a neurolinguistics training session when a fellow attendee approached me during a break and asked, "Are you the one who talks to animals?" I told him I was, and he then began to share with me about his dog, Lucy, and asked if I could help with an issue he was having with her.

He explained that he would take Lucy to a local off-leash dog spot so she could socialize with other dogs. However, instead of playing with dogs, she'd move from person to person for attention and scratches. When I connected with Lucy, I felt her "princess" energy and confidence. I assumed she was a small dog because she presented herself to me as petite and mentioned that her owner took her everywhere. To my surprise, when he showed me a picture, she was a beautiful Australian Shepherd, and she was not small!

Lucy's owner wanted her to play with other dogs. She told me, "I'm not scared of them." When I asked the owner if she seemed scared, he said no; she seemed confident but only interested in getting attention from people at the park. Lucy explained that she wasn't uninterested in other dogs; she just didn't know how to play, so she preferred interacting with people.

It turned out that Lucy had been a "people dog" most of her life, often even going to restaurants where her owner would order her an unseasoned steak, and she would eat at the same time. She went everywhere with him and only started socializing with dogs this way a little later in life. Lucy didn't feel like she was missing out; she was having a blast at the park with all the "dog people." They would talk to her, compliment her, and pet her. She was used to being the center of attention! To her, the issue was a difference in perspective between her and her owner. If she didn't see it as a problem, then, in her mind, why would she need to change?

I shared my insights with the owner and informed him that I wasn't a dog trainer, so I couldn't provide professional advice on Lucy's behavior. I suggested that if he wanted to explore it further, he could contact a qualified professional in that field. Today, they continue to live a full life together, with Lucy happily soaking up attention wherever she goes.

A Simple Fix: Leo, the Barking Dog

Leo's owners reached out to me for a session to discuss his incessant barking at the door when packages were delivered. They said it was difficult to get him to stop once he started. When I asked Leo about it, he said, "Well, it works, doesn't it?" He explained that when someone came to the door, he barked, and they went away. In his mind, his barking achieved the desired result, though, in reality, the delivery person was dropping off a package and leaving.

I empathized with Leo's perspective and explained that the delivery driver would leave the package whether or not he barked. Still, Leo insisted that he wanted to alert his owners when people came to the door and that it was his job. I suggested to his owners that a dog trainer could provide more detailed help at home if they did not like the continuation of the behavior or the root cause behind it. In the meantime, we agreed on a compromise: Leo could alert them, but once acknowledged, he needed to be quiet.

Understanding how animals process language, I taught them to avoid phrases like "Don't bark." Such phrases can confuse the dogs because, more than likely, what happens is that our unconscious mind sends an image of the dog barking, as our unconscious doesn't immediately process negatives. This can accidentally perpetuate the very thing we are asking them not to do.

Instead, I advised them to use positive language to reinforce the thing we want them to do, such as saying, "Thank you, Leo. You can be quiet now."

Weeks later, the owners reported that this new routine was working well. It was a simple solution with immediate results, effective because everyone agreed and followed through.

A Complex Case: Rocco and Leia Overcoming the Odds

A student and client of mine, Kerri, requested a session for her two dogs, Rocco and Leia. She and her husband had adopted Rocco first and then, more recently, Leia. Unfortunately, the two dogs were not getting along and had to be separated in the house. Rocco had an issue with resource guarding, and he shared with me that he'd had a challenging past in which he'd struggled for resources and, because of this, didn't understand how to make friends. He'd seen other dogs as a threat to the limited resources he had. He also mentioned that he'd been working with a dog trainer and was loving it!

Kerri mentioned Leia would join the training sessions soon. Leia had been brought in as a stray with a similar history of fighting for resources and also did not understand how to make friends. Even though both dogs struggled with this, they shared the desire for companionship and needed help to get there.

In our first session, Rocco said, "I see dogs on the TV with friends all the time, and I wonder how they do it!" For those who might be reading this and wondering why he was having issues with Leia, you have to understand that while he might be interested, his body had still created habits and reinforced certain instincts that had served him at one time to help him survive. In cases like this, we have to help the animal teach their mind and body that these situations are safe and okay.

Together, we came up with a plan to work through these issues so the two dogs could create a long-lasting friendship. Since this case was a complex one, we all agreed that we would make sure a professional dog trainer was in the mix, something I call "the Dream Team." That way, I could use certain techniques to help the dogs release old emotional baggage at the unconscious level, communicating with them through the process to keep them in the loop with the trainer and make sure they were following the steps that would bring them together. On the physical front, the dog trainer would help them learn new habits and coping skills.

After our first communication session, we immediately went to work. That first session was the hardest because the dogs were either going to agree to work together or not. They made the first step by agreeing to do the work necessary for a peaceful and happy home life. I did their first emotional clearing session to release unwanted trapped emotions and give their unconscious minds emotionally clean slates—this would give them a mental leg up by the time they got to the trainer.

On our second call, Kerri began by sharing the news that the two of them had had an accidental run-in with each other inside the home. They had not yet been reunited due to the resource issues and advice from the trainer that they were not yet ready. Not to mention, the run-in had occurred in Rocco's most defensive spot in the home, the kitchen.

Kerri shared with me that the dogs had made no attempt at one another, and while she'd immediately separated them, there'd been no altercation. This was a huge step in the right direction. When I began that session, Rocco started and said, "In the spirit of transformation, I'll let Leia go first." Leia came in and immediately began to express how proud of them she was for the unexpected visit in the kitchen, especially because she came in "ablaze." She shared that she'd rushed in, and "it could have been really intimidating, but he [Rocco] handled it like a pro."

Kerri mentioned that they had an annual vacation coming up. They would take a long road trip in a camper vehicle across the state to Grandpa's house on the East Coast. Once there, Rocco would stay with Grandpa while Kerri and her husband traveled out of the country.

Originally, the plan was to have Leia stay behind for safety purposes for the dogs, as they weren't sure how they'd do in small quarters where they wouldn't be able to be separated unless they were in crates. On this second call, Rocco was the one to propose the possibility of Leia joining them, communicating that he thought they were ready.

Everyone kept up the hard work, and they all went on the trip. It was the start of the most beautiful friendship. Not only did Rocco and Leia become close companions who adventured together, snuggled together, and loved each other, but Rocco even started playing with other dogs. This journey opened him up tremendously in many ways. I even received a video of them with Grandpa's dog, Lucy, enjoying the sun together on their East Coast trip. They lived happily ever after until Rocco passed away in August 2023.

Honoring Rocco's Memory: My Favorite Rocco Moments

- "Do you see how sweet my eyes are?" This was Rocco's opening line in session one, showing me his big, kind brown eyes.
- "I think it would be fun if someday we could go to the lake together and get in the water." From session one, after opening up to the possibility of friendship with Leia. By "the lake," he was referring to the ocean.
- "This could be a really fun next chapter in my life, and I'm going to try and consider it to be that way." From session one.
- "I'm the OG Good Boy... Tell Dad to call me that!" From session two, proud after a successful accidental greeting with Leia.
- "Thank you so much for the opportunity of growth... It wasn't something I was expecting, and it was something I was nervous about, but I'm really glad it's happening. I didn't understand how good the prospect of having a life partner could be." From session two, directed at Kerri, about the work with Leia and the trainer.

Rocco's journey from struggle to joy is a testament to the power of understanding, patience, and love. It is my hope that his memory and story with Leia will inspire you. He reminds us that with compassion and dedication, even the most challenging obstacles can be overcome. His spirit and transformation will forever be a beacon of hope and encouragement to all who face challenges and strive to open their hearts to love.

What We Learned in Chapter 3:

- Animals communicate telepathically through pictures, words, and feelings, often in an unconscious, natural way, with the ability to control this communication, switching it on or off as needed, exemplified by birds' coordinated flight and predators' silent hunting.

- Our ability to receive information, including telepathic messages, depends on our openness and receptiveness, which can be improved by consciously choosing to remain open and embracing life fully, leading to enhanced intuitive capacities and better communication with animals.

- Becoming a skilled animal communicator involves learning to accurately interpret incoming information, which often includes abstract images or impressions. With practice and self-awareness, one can differentiate between personal thoughts and external messages. Asking questions silently or out loud during sessions helps facilitate the flow of information, and documenting messages quickly prevents conscious interference. Practice without pressure and maintain humility, as varying clarity levels require ongoing interpretation and adjustment.

- Resolving animal communication cases varies in complexity, often requiring addressing unrealistic owner expectations, seeking professional training, investigating potential medical issues, and considering cognitive impairments in animals. Effective solutions involve educating owners, creating collaborative plans, and sometimes consulting veterinarians or trainers to ensure the well-being of both the animal and the owner.

CHAPTER 4

Dynamics of Animal Communication

Animal communication is not about interpreting behavioral cues or making educated guesses. Instead, it taps into the intuitive connections that exist between all living beings using telepathic and energetic exchanges to talk with our non-human friends. It's about stepping into a space of openness, inviting us to listen and share, to give and receive clarity and understanding directly to and from the animals. Language is the primary element in human communication. We use words to express our thoughts, emotions, and desires. Animals have their own ways of communicating with each other, from vocalizations to body language and beyond.

Animal communicators adopt various methods that match animals' unique communication styles, offering diverse ways to connect with them. No one method is superior to another! Even though clients might have a favorite way to participate, every approach has its benefits. The key is finding the method that allows for the best connection between the communicator and the animal. Sessions can be private, live on the phone, through video chat, or even a mix of both. A communicator is connecting with the energetic body of the animal, not the physical body, so distance is no object. The animal does not need to be present for the session, and the communicator does not need to be physically next to them.

Here are the two main ways an animal communicator may conduct a session.

Privately Conducted Sessions

A private session allows an animal communicator to connect with an animal through a photograph and details provided beforehand, often without the owner's presence. This type of session can facilitate a clear connection without distractions so the animal communicator can produce the best results.

Live Sessions: In-Person or Virtual

Live sessions can be highly dynamic, with the communicator engaging in real-time with the animal and owner. This allows for instant feedback and encourages a deeper, three-way conversation, creating a rich interaction and understanding.

The caveat is the need for an open and willing owner, as they play an integral role as a live participant. An owner's receptiveness and trust in the process significantly impact the session's overall effectiveness. They are not just passive observers but active collaborators whose energy and openness can significantly enhance the communicative flow between the animal and the communicator. In this shared space, skepticism or closed-mindedness can create barriers, whereas openness fosters an environment where profound insights and meaningful exchanges flourish.

Some basic information is usually collected before starting a session to help make the process smoother. Here's what's typically gathered.

Picture of the Animal

A recent photo of the animal, whether they are still with us or have passed on, helps the communicator focus and connect with the animal's spirit. Details in the picture—such as seeing a full view of the face—may also help strengthen the energetic connection.

Name of the Animal

Having the animal's name lets the communicator speak to them directly, which is crucial for building a connection and making sure the animal knows the session is for them. This is particularly important if there's more than one animal in the session, as it ensures the communication is with the correct one. `

Age of the Animal

Knowing the animal's age helps the communicator understand which stage of life they might be in, affecting how deeply and in what way they communicate. It also helps make sense of the messages received. For instance, younger animals may communicate in a lively manner, whereas older animals might be calmer, slower, or even communicate less, possibly showing signs of aging in their cognitive abilities.

General Location

Some communicators, especially those who are more visually oriented, may benefit from knowing where the animal lives. Imagining an energetic link to the animal in its general location can convince the unconscious mind of the connection, reinforcing a stronger connection for the session.

Collecting this information up front is an essential step for a successful animal communication session, leading to clearer and more effective interactions that benefit both the animal and the human involved. Depending on what the session aims to achieve, the communicator may need additional details. For instance, if I'm helping a client with a dog that reacts strongly on walks, I'd want to know if they've seen a professional dog trainer. I'd also like to see if the owner is open to this idea (I'll talk more about this later in the book).

The Role of the Owner

Successful animal communication sessions rely on effective collaboration between three key participants: the animal, the communicator, and the pet owner. To achieve the best results, all parties need to work in harmony. Pet owners should approach these sessions as a team effort, especially if they're conducted live, keeping an open mind and being ready to actively participate alongside the communicator and their pet if or when needed.

Consider this perspective: Animals are highly sensitive to their owner's energy, often looking to them as the leader of their pack. If an owner is skeptical or closed off, their pet may mirror this attitude toward the communicator, making it challenging for the communicator to establish a connection. In some cases, this skepticism can even prevent any meaningful dialogue with the animal altogether. On the flip side, when an owner is receptive, their pet is more likely to be cooperative and engage in the sessions.

While an owner's positive attitude is always helpful, it doesn't override an animal's inherent personality traits. For example, a naturally shy animal may still be hesitant and require more time to warm up, even if their owner is completely open to the process. An animal with a confident and outgoing nature might engage more quickly and with a bit more energy. However, the energy an owner brings to the session also greatly affects the flow of communication, highlighting the importance of respecting and adapting to each animal's unique temperament and comfort level.

Common Types of Sessions

1. Rainbow Bridge Sessions

Rainbow bridge sessions are designed for animals who have passed away and transitioned into spirit. These sessions offer a unique opportunity for pet owners to connect with their beloved departed animals, helping them understand how they are now and what their transitioning experience was like. For many, this connection can be profoundly comforting and healing, especially when the passing was unexpected or sudden.

During a rainbow bridge session, owners often have questions that range from seeking closure regarding their animal's well-being in the afterlife to specific questions about their happiness, comfort, favorite memories, and ways they can still look for their presence. The goal of these sessions is not only to reconnect family members and provide answers but also to help owners find peace and closure, reassuring them that their pet is safe, happy, and at peace on the other side.

These sessions can be deeply emotional and transformative. Many owners report a sense of relief and comfort after hearing from their departed pets, knowing that they are still connected through the eternal bond of love.

2. Lost Animal Sessions

These sessions aim to locate missing animals. Due to the complexity involved, some communicators may not take on these cases. Lost animals are often scared and disoriented, which makes it challenging to gather precise information. Communicators typically conduct these sessions privately with the animal to avoid the emotional influence of the owner and allow for the most accurate and clear information.

The first step is usually to determine if the lost animal is still alive or has passed away, which is especially relevant if they've been missing for a while. This information should be shared cautiously, as emotions can influence the session. The communicator tunes into the animal's feelings first; those who are kinesthetic might feel a floating sensation if the animal has passed.

Next, the communicator may ask the animal to describe what they feel under their feet. If the animal mentions feeling grass, cold dirt, or other textures, it suggests they may still be alive. The communicator should then ask the animal to describe any landmarks or location details that they can share with the owner. If the animal expresses a floating sensation or cannot describe anything tangible, it may indicate that they have crossed over. In that case, follow-up questions may provide closure to the owner.

Handling these sessions delicately is crucial, and having multiple communicators verify the same information can increase reliability. If the communicator is confident that the animal is alive, immediate action is vital, as time is of the essence in these situations. Instincts may cause the animal to move despite instructions to stay put, so locating a lost animal requires dedicated effort from both the communicator and the owner. Effective lost animal communication involves quickly acting on gathered information and having people on the ground search for landmarks as soon as possible.

3. End-of-Life Preparation Sessions

End-of-life preparation sessions are designed for older animals or those nearing the end of their life. These sessions provide a meaningful opportunity for both the owners and their pets to cherish memories and discuss how to make the most of their remaining time together.

During these sessions, owners can reminisce about favorite moments, adventures, and milestones shared with their pets. They can discuss ways to keep the pet comfortable, such as preferred sleeping arrangements, favorite foods, or soothing activities. Understanding any preferences the pet may have regarding their end-of-life care is also important, whether it's spending time outside, being surrounded by family, or listening to calming music. Preparing emotionally for the farewell ensures the pet feels loved and appreciated until the very end. Finally, these sessions can help owners consider how they want to remember and honor their pets after they have passed, whether through keepsakes, memorials, or rituals.

4. Health-Compromised Sessions

Health-compromised sessions provide animals with a way to express their health issues. It is crucial to understand that these sessions are not a substitute for professional veterinary care. A veterinarian should always verify any health-related information obtained during the session.

These sessions are particularly helpful when an animal is experiencing discomfort or pain and the source of the issue is unknown or unclear. The role of the animal communicator in these sessions is to give the animal a voice, allowing them to express how they are feeling in their body and how they'd like support.

For instance, in one session with a dog named Rooster, he communicated that he had a toothache on the upper left side of his mouth. The owner was unaware of this issue but took him to the vet after the session. The veterinarian confirmed the toothache and extracted the problematic tooth, and Rooster healed quickly.

Sometimes, we may discuss an already diagnosed issue to gain the animal's perspective, keep them in the loop regarding what the vet said, and help them understand their treatment plan. This may be especially helpful for animals who are tricky to give meds to.

These sessions can be invaluable in involving the animal in the conversation regarding their own health issues and providing owners with insights that allow them to see their animal's perspective. By listening to the animal, owners can better understand their pets' needs and ensure they receive appropriate care.

Challenges with Personal Pets

Communicating with one's pet can be surprisingly tricky for beginners due to pre-existing emotional bonds and expectations. It's also challenging because of the deep and natural relationship we have with our pets, often leading us to mistake their telepathic messages for our thoughts. To develop your skills and confidence, it is sometimes best to initially work with animals you are not familiar with. As you enhance your abilities, communicating with your own animals will become easier! However, even the best animal communicators sometimes seek help from other communicators for their pets. This is because our emotional connection with our pets can cloud our judgment, making it challenging to receive information clearly.

An example of this is when I was doing a session with a miniature horse named Toby. In our session, Toby shared with me that he'd like to be taken on walks around the neighborhood. When I shared this information with one of his owners, Linda, she laughed and said that her husband recently shared that he wanted to take Toby on walks. Well, that wasn't the husband's idea at all. What happened is that her husband telepathically picked up the idea from Toby and mistook it for his own thoughts. This is a common occurrence for owners and their animals.

Practicing with animals you do not have a personal bond with can provide a confidence boost, as it allows you to verify information that would otherwise be outside your knowledge base. It is much more of a confidence boost to get something correct and think, *Wow! There is no way I could have known that about this animal.* Whereas, with our own pets, it would be easy to think, *Of course, I got that because I know them so well already.* By working with unfamiliar animals, you're more likely to reinforce the accuracy and reliability of your abilities. You learn to trust your intuition and telepathic skills more, as you must rely solely on these aspects to establish a connection and communicate effectively.

Interacting with a variety of animals exposes you to a wide range of personalities, behaviors, and communication styles. Each animal is unique, and this diversity enriches your understanding and abbreviation of the nuanced nature of animal communication. You'll learn to adapt to different temperaments and preferences, which can enhance your ability to communicate in many different situations.

Additionally, practicing with unknown or less familiar animals provides a valuable learning experience. It reveals that the communication process is not always within your control, and your abilities can vary from one animal to another. This humbling realization keeps you open-minded and teaches you to approach these sessions with a fresh perspective, encouraging continuous growth and improvement in your skills.

Communicating Across Domesticated Lines

Domestic animals, accustomed to human interaction, often bring a wealth of human-centered context into communication sessions. They are sometimes more open to connecting with communicators and sharing their personal experiences. For instance, if a session is scheduled, the animal may sense it from their owner and greet the communicator with an "I knew you were coming" attitude. Repeat clients often find their animals waiting with an agenda, eager to share updates like a recent move, new training, or a family pregnancy. These animals can also pick up on many labels, such as alarm clocks, videos, and even colors. Their ability to absorb information from our environment is truly remarkable.

On the other hand, communicating with wildlife, when possible, offers a deeply profound experience. These animals are intimately connected with the natural world and bring perspectives that encourage a deeper relationship with our environment. Wild animals often provide wisdom and insights that go beyond our human-centered understanding of the world. However, when they are not available for conversation, they may not answer you or may say they're busy, which is why I stated that domesticated animals are sometimes more available.

For example, I was once out walking a trail and noticed a large bird perched in a tree. I was so excited to tune in and communicate with it. Whenever I connect, I first say, "Hello, my name is Alex. I would love to chat with you. Are you available?" I want to make sure that I am kind and polite and ask permission. The bird simply replied, "Not right now. I am hunting."

I find that if I catch a wild animal in the middle of doing something important in their environment, they may not have time for chit-chat. Domesticated animals, however, are almost always ready, available, and prepared. If you are lucky enough to catch an animal in the wild that is open and available, you're in for a magnificent treat. Engaging in communication with wildlife not only broadens our appreciation for all living things that exist in this world but also deepens our connection to the planet we all share.

From Earth Side to Spirit Side

Earth Side Animals

When communicating with animals that share our world, the dialogue often centers on their present physical experiences. I make it a point to let the animal lead the conversation in each session. This not only helps us build a connection and rapport energetically but also opens the floor for the animals to express what is most pressing for them.

Unpredictability is part of magic! Every animal brings a unique perspective. Some are eager to explore a wide range of topics, while others might quickly voice a specific concern or invite questions from their owner. As mentioned before, in these conversations, animals may reveal insights about their physical well-being, including any discomfort or pain they're experiencing, activities they crave more of, or even specific dietary preferences and requests. This invaluable information allows us to better understand their needs and desires, ensuring we can provide a life that's not only comfortable but also enriching for them.

Bandit, the Chattiest Dog

I fondly remember a fun session where a client gave her dog, Bandit, an entire hour to express whatever he wished. At first, the idea of navigating an hour without specific questions from the owner made me wonder if we could keep it engaging the entire time. However, my concerns quickly vanished as Bandit proved to be an excellent communicator, full of insights and stories that could have filled hours. He touched on various topics with the enthusiasm only the most spirited dog can muster. One surprising request was for his owner's mother to paint his portrait as a Christmas gift. When I shared this request with his owner, she told me that her mom was an artist.

A particularly funny moment came when Bandit sent me an image of his toes in the sunlight and said loudly, "They're hot!" I initially thought he might be indicating discomfort from hot pavements during walks or something of that nature. To clarify, I asked Bandit what he meant. It turned out he loved the warmth of the sun on his toes during sunbathing sessions, a favorite activity his owner later confirmed with numerous photos that she sent me.

As our session neared its end, Bandit suggested a night walk to celebrate his owner's "recent achievement." When his owner hesitated due to safety concerns, Bandit humorously asked, "Why? Is she afraid we'll run into… *bandits?*" This clever play on words not only made us laugh but also revealed the backstory of his name, inspired by his puppy antics of stealing bathroom rugs and running off with them.

The session was a delightful exploration of Bandit's physical world, filled with humor, warmth, and unexpected wisdom. Of course, when I asked the owner at the end what chatty mix of dog breeds he is, she told me that he is a Husky mix. I couldn't help but laugh once more, thinking, "Yes, of course he's a Husky!"

Animals in Spirit

Conversing with animals in spirit entails a unique form of communication. While they might recall physical memories, their focus often shifts to their transition and experiences in the afterlife, offering insights beyond the earthly realm. Animals in spirit frequently share loving messages with their owners, expressing gratitude for the life they shared. These messages often revolve around cherished activities, favorite foods, or shared adventures.

A significant aspect of these conversations is providing closure for the owner and supporting their healing journey. The animals in spirit seek to comfort their human companions by affirming their enduring bond and continued presence. They often suggest specific signs or ways for their owners to recognize them in the physical world, such as unusual animal sightings, specific scents, or even dreams. By doing so, they reassure their owners that they are still connected and watching over them.

Animals who have transitioned to the spirit side exhibit a fascinating diversity in how they communicate their experiences after passing and express gratitude. Not all animals prioritize the same topics in their spiritual communications. For instance, while some may share their appreciation for the ways their human companions honored their memory, others who lived for adventure and play might express gratitude by highlighting shared joyful activities of their enduring adventurous spirit.

A question that surfaces frequently in the realm of animal communication is whether animals have preferences regarding the handling of their physical remains. It's a deeply emotional topic for many pet owners seeking to honor their beloved companions in the best way possible. Interestingly, direct preferences from animals on this matter are not as common as we might think. More commonly, animals express a wish for their humans to choose whatever path promotes their healing and closure.

This approach offers us profound spiritual insight: From their vantage point, death is not an end but a transformation. They reassure us that even though they have shed their earthly form, they remain an active, loving presence in our lives. This perspective soothes the heartache of loss, emphasizing that while we may perceive death as a permanent separation, our spirit companions are never truly far away. They continue to watch over and support us from the other side.

Zola's Message from Heaven

In one particularly resonant session with a repeat client, I reconnected with their beloved dog, Zola, who had recently transitioned. Zola's spirit was vibrant, almost buzzing with energy, a stark contrast to her last chapter on Earth when she battled multiple health issues and struggled with mobility.

Her excitement to communicate was evident. She eagerly shared how liberated she felt, free from the physical constraints that had once limited her.

The grieving owners, longing for a sign of Zola's continued presence, asked how they might recognize her reaching out from the other side. "Look for me in the ladybugs," Zola conveyed. Such a specific message intrigued us, yet how it would manifest remained a mystery. This is a fairly common occurrence with animals in spirits and the sometimes abstract nature of their messages.

The session concluded with our hearts touched by Zola's message and excited to see her sign come through. Remarkably, it wasn't long before the profound significance of Zola's words unfolded. Stepping outside, my clients were greeted by an unexpected visitor, a ladybug, who audaciously flew directly into one of their faces. The symbolism was unmistakable. This wasn't just a ladybug but a loving nudge from Zola following our session, a spirited assurance that she was joyous, free, and forever intertwined with their lives.

This touching encounter was a heartwarming confirmation of life's continuance beyond the physical realm, proving the power of our animals in spirit and their ability to connect with us through the most delicate of signs.

Giovani's Message in the Clouds

I had the honor of connecting again with a profoundly wise Shih Tzu named Giovanni, who had recently crossed over into the spirit realm. Giovanni had a deeply nurturing bond with his human family, offering them comfort and companionship throughout his earthly life. As we ventured into our conversation, Giovanni conveyed a message destined to soothe the piercing hearts of the grieving family. "Find me in the clouds," he softly instructed.

This guidance, while mystifying at first, bloomed into a profound experience sometime later. My client was at an outdoor concert and found her gaze drifting up to the sky. There, amidst the vast blue expanse, a cloud formation caught her eye, one that unmistakably resembled the distinct features of a Shih Tzu. The alignment was so accurate, so filled with Giovanni's essence, that it left no room for doubt. She captured this serendipitous moment with a picture, which she later emailed to me to share. This image, more than just a visual representation, stood as a testament to Giovanni's promise.

What We Learned in Chapter 4:

- Before an animal communication session, basic info like a recent photo, the animal's name, age, and location is collected to help the communicator connect and understand the context. Additional details may be needed depending on the session's goals.

- Successful animal communication sessions need collaboration between the animal, communicator, and pet owner. An open-minded and positive attitude from the owner enhances the pet's engagement, though the pet's personality also significantly impacts the process.

- Common animal communication sessions include Rainbow Bridge Sessions for connecting with departed pets, Lost Animal Sessions to locate missing pets, End-of-Life Preparation Sessions to cherish memories and discuss comfort, and Health-Compromised Sessions to understand an animal's health issues, which should be verified by a veterinarian.

- Communicating with one's own pet is challenging due to emotional bonds and expectations, making it hard to distinguish messages. Beginners should practice with unfamiliar animals to boost confidence, as even experienced communicators sometimes seek outside help for clarity.

- Communicating with domestic animals is easier due to their familiarity with humans, while connecting with wildlife offers profound insights but is more challenging. Domestic animals eagerly share updates, whereas wild animals may be too busy. Engaging with both deepens our appreciation and connection to the natural world.

- Communicating with animals in spirit involves sharing their afterlife experiences and comforting their owners. These conversations offer closure, with animals suggesting signs of their presence. They emphasize that death is a transformation, not an end, and continue to support and love from the other side.

CHAPTER 5

Inner-World Reflections

I n the vastness of communication, where words are merely vessels, we find a profound truth: Our internal landscapes shape our interactions in powerful ways. This is especially true in the art of animal communication, where language goes beyond words and enters the telepathic realm. In this chapter, we'll explore how our inner world significantly impacts the quality and authenticity of our communication with animals.

Perception Is Projection

The saying "perception is projection" means that the world we experience is a reflection of our internal state. Our perceptions are the lens through which we interpret our reality. They form our individual truth. Nowhere is this more evident than in the world of animal communication.

Consider this scenario. You dislike swimming, and during a communication session, the animal unexpectedly expresses a similar sentiment. This synchronicity begs the question: Is it truly the animal's preference, or is it your perception shaping the exchange? This is why it is so important for animal communicators to have a heightened state of awareness over their own emotional clarity and neutrality so that we can capture the essence of the message without the interface of our own bias.

The Impact of Beliefs and Emotions

We carry with us an array of beliefs and emotions that can either enrich or obstruct our reality and understanding of information in an animal communication session. Unresolved feelings and deeply rooted negative beliefs may create mental clutter, forming a veil over the raw information we seek to receive. This clutter can block the free flow of telepathic information and muddy the waters of our intuitive sessions. It can also sway the information, leading us to mistranslate it based on our judgments and perceptions.

Drawing on principles from psychology and personal development, we understand that clearing this clutter, these entrenched beliefs and emotional debris, is essential for accessing undistorted messages. You must metaphorically leave your "stuff" at the door to step into a space conducive to collecting pure, unfiltered information.

For clear communication, especially in the subtle world of animal connection, it's essential to recognize our inherent human nature. Rather than seeking perfection, this pursuit is about nurturing awareness to release mental and emotional blockages that hinder our understanding and connection.

The essence of this practice lies in recognizing that despite our best efforts, complete accuracy in communication is an ideal, not always a reality. We are, after all, human! We are creatures of emotion, bias, and imperfection. And there is nothing wrong with that. This acknowledgment does not dampen our potential for profound connection. Rather, it grounds us in humility and fosters a compassionate approach toward improvement. It teaches us that the path to clearer communication with our animal companions is a continuous journey of self-awareness and growth.

By aspiring for the highest possible accuracy, we cultivate patience, empathy, and a deeper resonance with the beings we seek to understand. Our limiting decisions, otherwise known as our limiting beliefs, often stem from past experiences and internalized ideas from a young age. Like many things in life, our limiting decisions can sometimes get in the way of our goals. In this case, they can get in the way of becoming a fluid and confident animal communicator. These are decisions we make at an unconscious level to take on a belief that puts constraints on our abilities, telling us what we can and cannot do or who we can and cannot be. They form an invisible barrier around our potential, fueling doubts like *I am not good enough* or *I can't connect like others do.* You can delete those from your mind as soon as you read them.

For someone seeking to bridge the gap between human and animal minds, these beliefs act as noise, distorting the clarity and flow of telepathic communication. Recognizing and challenging these limiting decisions is a helpful step toward unlocking your full communication potential. It is about transforming the narrative from one of self-imposed limitations to one of empowerment and reminding ourselves of the boundless capacity for growth, connection, and understanding nestled within us. In doing so, we not only enhance our communion with the animal world but also create a great sense of inner freedom and possibility for life in general.

I tell my students, "If it has to do with us, it has to do with them." This mantra showcases the interconnectedness of personal development and enhanced communication skills. The essence of this principle is straightforward: The deeper we venture into our own growth and self-improvement, the more capable we become in every facet of life, including our ability to connect with and understand animals.

The symbiotic relationship between self-evolution and animal communication is pivotal. As we refine our sense of self, shedding layers of preconceptions and emotional baggage, we not only elevate our own existence in this human experience but also pave the way for a rich and fulfilling life as an animal communicator. I am extremely passionate about this topic—can you tell? If you focus on this as much as you do your communication skills, it will change everything.

Tools for Transformation

The exploration of personal development tools is crucial for anyone looking to deepen their connection with animals. This step is often overlooked and missed in the animal communication world, but focusing on it will get you to your goals much faster. These tools not only facilitate a deepened awareness of one's internal world but also play a significant role in nurturing a state of relaxation and availability in both body and mind that is conducive to enhancing intuitive skills.

There is no "one size fits all" regarding the best methods and tools to use. Rather, some will resonate with you more than others. It depends on your personal preferences, experiences, and, of course, beliefs.

Below, I have outlined some of our favorite tools for guiding students through their journey. I share this to help and support you along your journey, too.

Meditation

Meditation is a powerful practice that promotes relaxation and well-being for both the body and the mind. By incorporating meditation into your routine, you can experience a myriad of benefits that extend beyond personal development and reach into the realm of intuitive animal communication. Meditation is known to reduce stress and promote relaxation by calming the mind and soothing the nervous system. Through focused breathing and mindfulness techniques, you can release physical tension, lower blood pressure, and improve overall bodily functions. The state of relaxation not only fosters a sense of peace and tranquility but also contributes to better physical health. Talk about helping and assisting us with cultivating a sense of emotional neutrality!

As a personal development tool, meditation enhances self-awareness, emotional regulation, and mental clarity. It cultivates a heightened sense of intuition and empathy, allowing people to connect more deeply with themselves and others. This heightened awareness and attunement to emotions and subtle cues can be invaluable when engaging in animal communication, enabling practitioners to better understand and respond to the needs and signs of non-verbal beings.

When people practice meditation to relax and sharpen their intuition, they are better equipped to engage in intuitive animal communication. By cultivating a calm and receptive state of mind through meditation, practitioners can establish a more profound connection with animals, interpreting their behaviors, emotions, and nonverbal cues with heightened sensitivity and understanding. This, in turn, facilitates more meaningful and effective communication with animal companions.

Are you new to meditation? Not to worry. It's important to remember that meditation is not about achieving an empty mind, especially when it comes to animal communication. Having some type of activity in the brain is actually really important. Even for those who are new to meditation or active thoughts, practice can still offer valuable benefits.

Instead of striving for complete mental silence, meditation involves simply acknowledging and gently redirecting thoughts. Over time, meditation can help people find moments of calm and clarity amidst the busyness of the mind, ultimately leading to a greater sense of peace and well-being.

Breathwork

Research indicates that breathwork practices offer numerous benefits for nervous system regulation and emotional well-being. By gaining control of one's breath, you can positively influence your autonomic nervous system, leading to reduced stress and anxiety levels. The practice of breathwork can facilitate emotional neutrality, allowing you to respond to situations with increased composure and clarity.

This enhanced emotional regulation and nervous system balance can be particularly advantageous for those learning animal communication, as it enables practitioners to approach interactions with animals from a grounded and centered state. Additionally, the ability to regulate one's breath and emotions through breathwork can foster a deeper connection and understanding when engaging in intuitive communication with animal companions.

Journaling: Unlocking Unwanted, Negative Beliefs

In our continuous quest for personal transformation and deeper connection with the animals we treasure, the power of journaling cannot be overstated. It is a nurturing practice that not only allows us to converse with our inner selves but also serves as a potent catalyst for change.

With this understanding, here is a methodical approach designed to guide you through the intricate landscape of your beliefs, particularly those that hinder your potential. This process, deeply insightful and empowering, will help you identify, challenge, and ultimately transform the limiting decisions that cloud your mind and obstruct your communication channels with animals. Each step of this process is an invitation to introspection and self-discovery, encouraging you to dig beneath the surface of your conscious mind to uncover and address the beliefs that have silently shaped your reality.

By engaging with this journaling tool, you empower yourself to clear the clutter of mental and emotional obstacles, paving the path towards a liberated, more insightful existence. Whether it's the belief that you are not skilled enough to connect with animals on a deeper level or the fear of not being understood, this journaling process is here to help you rewrite the narrative of your life, turning limiting decisions into stepping stones for growth and profound connection.

Limiting Belief Solution: A Journaling Prompt

1. Identify and write down the unwanted belief. A negative or un-
    wanted belief is one that feels disempowering.

    _____

    _____

    _____

2. With this unwanted belief in mind, what causes you to believe it?

    _____

    _____

    _____

3. Where did this belief come from? If unsure, ask your unconscious
    mind, _If I knew where I got it from, where would that be?_

    _____

    _____

    _____

6. What benefits do you gain by keeping this belief?

    _____

    _____

    _____

7. What are the costs of maintaining this belief now, and what will they be in a year? Take your time and be as descriptive as possible.

_____

_____

_____

8. Does everyone share this belief, or have you ever found it to be untrue? If so, when?

_____

_____

_____

9. If you decide to release this belief, what positive feeling or belief would you like to have or feel instead?

_____

_____

_____

10. How would embracing this new belief change your life for the better? What positive things would happen as a result of this new truth?

_____

_____

_____

11. Choose! Write down the new desired belief in *present* tense. For example, "I am unstoppable!"

_____

_____

_____

12. What immediate action can you take to embody this new belief? Are you able to do that now?

_____

_____

_____

By engaging in self-awareness and applying the tools offered, you fulfill your responsibility to remove barriers and open yourself up for a true exchange. When we have decluttered our unresolved emotions and beliefs that disempower us, we can more easily enter the field of love-consciousness that supports animal communication. Thus, I encourage you to practice with diligence. In the end, it is not just about what we communicate but the purity with which we convey it.

What We Learned in Chapter 5:

- "Perception is projection" means our experiences reflect our internal state, making it essential for animal communicators to maintain emotional clarity and neutrality to avoid projecting their own biases into the animal's messages.
- Our beliefs and emotions can enrich or obstruct animal communication. Unresolved feelings create mental clutter, blocking telepathic

information and leading to mistranslations. Clearing these beliefs is vital for clear communication. Recognizing our human imperfections fosters humility and continuous self-awareness, improving our connection with animals. Challenging limiting beliefs unlocks our full potential, enhancing both our understanding of animals and our overall life experience.

- Personal development tools are crucial for deepening animal communication. Tools like meditation, breathwork, and journaling enhance self-awareness and intuitive skills. There is no "one size fits all" approach; find what resonates with you. Clearing unresolved emotions and beliefs enables a true exchange and supports love-consciousness for effective communication. Practice diligently to convey your messages with clarity and purity.

CHAPTER 6

Initiating Animal Communication

Welcome to Chapter 6, where animal communication becomes more tangible. In this chapter, I'll guide you through a practical process to connect with animal consciousness. This isn't just communication as you know it; it's a deeper exchange of energies that offers insights beyond words.

We'll break down the steps, and by the end of this chapter, you'll have a guide through the entire process. Here are my best tips for beginners:

1. It's normal to feel like you're talking to yourself at first, especially if you rely on your auditory senses. With practice, distinguishing between your thoughts and genuine communication will become clearer.

2. Keep meticulous notes of all the information you receive, including how it came through. Did you see an image, hear words, or feel a sensation? These details help you verify information later with the animal's owner.

3. Note which of your senses are stronger and which need more work. Everyone starts in the same place, so don't worry.

4. Embrace your imagination and allow it to play along as you practice. For now, focus on learning rather than being right.

There is no pressure to perform—this is just for fun. Don't get attached to any results; let the experience unfold naturally. When you feel the communication flow through your body more easily, you can then refine your skills. For now, let anything and everything flow freely as you begin to exercise your mind in a new way. Be an open receiver for incoming information, no matter what it is. This approach will lead you to success more quickly.

Here is a perfect example of why it is important not to discount any piece of information at the beginning and to write down everything you get. While one of our amazing students, Emma, was completing her group program with us, Animal Communication for Beginners (aka ACB), she was convinced she wasn't receiving any bit of accurate information. Her most recent practice session was with a miniature donkey named Wylie.

When we asked her what she did get, she reluctantly blurted out, "A bowl of spaghetti, and that can't be anything!" Kayla and I laughed because it was actually something big! You see, Emma's homework was to ask Wylie what his essence was and for him to share some of his favorite things. Food is one of Wylie's favorite things of all time, so much so that when you watch him eat, his eyes close a little, and his ears go back in total bliss and relaxation. It is the cutest thing you'll ever see. Better yet, he slurps up his hay like spaghetti.

Emma was receiving the information, but being new to working the muscle, her unconscious mind presented the incoming information as a symbol—a bowl of spaghetti—that would be easy for her to interpret. It was an absolutely brilliant and pivotal moment for her that opened the door to paying more attention to interpreting information coming through her unconscious mind.

Everyone is born with the ability to communicate in this way. It just depends on how your body does it best, and that is the first thing you have to figure out. What are the mechanics of your body, and how can you work those mechanics to put these things into practice in your favor to yield the best result?

While this type of communication may come more naturally to some, just like athletic abilities, the key to becoming skilled for anyone is devotion to practice. Books can guide you, but practical application and taking action are essential.

The Steps and the "Why" Behind Them

Step 1: Pick the Animal You Wish to Connect With

As mentioned previously, choosing an animal that is not yours and is somewhat unfamiliar to you is going to give you the most profound experience, one that you'll be less likely to second guess. Perhaps you can ask a trusted friend or family member for permission to connect with one of their animal companions. Be sure to get proper consent from the owner and (later in the practice) from the animal.

With your chosen animal in mind, you can either sit with a picture of them up in front of you or gaze at them during the experience, or you can simply imagine them in your mind's eye. During the experience, you will pretend or imagine they are sitting out in front of you.

Step 2: Picking a Physical Stimulus

Before proceeding to direct communication, you will want to craft and create a physical stimulus. This action is aimed at convincing your unconscious mind that you are about to build a surplus of life-force energy within your body. This will support you in your connection.

You can achieve this by gently jumping up and down, rubbing your hands on your legs, or simply rubbing your hands together briskly (which most of my students opt for as it's easy to do while sitting down). Physical engagement acts as a signal or a command to your unconscious mind, as well as the body of your spirit, that you are ready and open to connecting. Additionally, it serves as an unconscious command of the activity you'll be doing and that you mean business about it.

Step 3: Breathwork and Building Energy

Engage in the "ha" breath technique (from Chapter 2) to build life-force energy in the body. With each inhale, you will fill your body with this life-force energy, imagining it surging through every cell and extending into your magnetic field. On the exhale, imagine storing and preserving this energy in your body. At the same time, add your physical stimulants for four complete breaths. Together, the two activities will amplify the energy.

Following the fourth breath, release the physical stimulus and allow your body to relax comfortably while continuing your "ha" breathing and building energy. Continue your breathing exercise until you feel or imagine that your body is full of life-force energy from the bottoms of your feet all the way to the top of your head. Notice the sensations in your body as you do so. If at any point you get lightheaded or uncomfortable, discontinue the exercise and allow your breath to go back to its natural rhythm before reengaging.

Step 4: Connecting Heart to Heart or Mind to Mind

In the previous chapters, we talked about the importance of energy and breathwork. To initiate contact with your animal friends, you must begin by grounding yourself and finding a resonance within the shared energy field. When you make a connection, you will create an energy cord that goes from you to the animal. You can create one that goes from your heart to their heart or your third eye (the space in between your brows and forehead) to their third eye. The preference is yours. Neither is better than the other. Whichever feels best for you and creates the best results is the one that you should practice with. You may even try both and see which suits you best.

Once you reach this step, visualize the surplus of energy in your field collecting in your preferred connection space in your body. Feel the unconditional love that you have to share with this animal. This will permeate the connection between you and help the two of you connect at a deeper level.

Step 5: Crafting the Energetic Cord

In this step, you will bring your attention to the part of your body that you've chosen as your connection point, either the third eye or heart. On the next inhale, imagine taking in more life-force energy from your surroundings. On the exhale, you use your surplus of unconditional love energy to extend the energetic cord all the way to the animal in front of you. Each inhale takes in energy. On the exhale, use that energy to create a connection from you to them.

You might even think of it as if you are using this surplus of life-force energy that you've built up in your body to send it out as a gift to thank them for your connection today. This energetic cord connecting you two is the conduit of pure energy, the bridge upon which communication will flow. Continue your "ha" breath by sending this cord all the way out until you feel or have the intention that you are connected.

Once you connect, do your best to allow the experience to be exactly what it is, without judgment or expectation. Your only goal and intention is to simply feel an exchange of energy. Notice any sensations as you sit connected with them. Notice the sensations that arise in your body, the images you might be seeing in your mind, or any thoughts that randomly pop into your head. Simply have an awareness of these things.

Step 6: Share Your Gratitude and Disconnect

Once you have completed your practice, properly disconnect from the animal by thanking them in your mind for spending time with you. Then, either retract the energetic cord back into your body or imagine cutting it with a tool like scissors, a knife, or a sword. Visualize their energy returning to them and your energy returning to you. Finally, close your session, open your eyes, and come back into the room.

For your first few connections, repeat the process of connecting and sharing energy. When you're ready to add more steps, instead of just feeling the energy, ask in your mind for the animal to share their essence with you. This means asking them to reveal their personality traits or who they are as a soul. You might sense what it feels like to be near them or get impressions of their personality, whether they are goofy, playful, shy, or reserved. Write down everything that comes to mind and try to verify it with the owner.

You can continue adding steps from there. For example, after asking about their essence, you might ask about their favorite activities next time. When asking questions, imagine sending the question through the energetic cord to the animal. To help with this, you might visualize placing the question inside the cord, taking a deep breath, and using the exhale to push the question through the cord. Then, wait and be present for a response.

To deepen your animal communication abilities, focus on developing each of your "clair" senses. This will enhance your ability to receive and interpret messages from animals.

Kinesthetic Communication

Pay close attention to your physical sensations during interactions or intuitive impressions that come through as a sense of "knowing." Note any changes in temperature, tingling sensations, or emotional responses. These can provide insights into the animal's physical and emotional state. Pay attention to gut feelings or immediate impressions about how the animal feels, their personality, or activities they might enjoy. For example, looking at a dog and instantly sensing they are fun, joyful, and playful indicates your kinesthetic sense is active.

Visual Communication

Visual communicators should practice maintaining mental clarity and openness to receiving images. Practice visualizing scenes in vivid detail to help translate visual messages from animals into meaningful insights. Allow images to form naturally without force. During an animal communication session, write down or record any visuals you receive, even if they don't make immediate sense. Later, review these visuals to see how they fit together, or ask your unconscious mind for clarity.

Auditory Communication

To enhance auditory communication, focus on quieting the mind to better hear and distinguish between your thoughts and those of the animal. Listen to the silence between your thoughts, where subtle messages are often found. Sometimes, messages can come through quickly and loudly. Write down anything that pops into your mind, even if you suspect it's your own thoughts. The more you practice, the better you'll become at identifying genuine messages. Focusing on these different senses will help you deepen your animal communication abilities and more profoundly understand the animals' lives and messages.

If the information starts coming in quickly and it's hard to keep up by hand, try speaking into an audio recorder. This allows your unconscious mind to gather information without your conscious mind filtering it out. Messages that come in quickly are often the most reliable because they are unfiltered.

Be patient with yourself and trust the process, as each session will bring you closer to mastering the language of animal communication. Embrace each step as a valuable learning experience, and remember that every bit of progress is significant. Stay committed to practicing regularly, and make use of all the tools and techniques provided.

Believe in your ability to connect deeply with animals and understand their messages. Consistency and dedication will pay off over time, and you'll find your skills improving steadily. Celebrate your progress, no matter how small it may seem, and keep pushing forward. Your efforts are building a profound, intuitive bond with your animal friends.

Through patience and persistence, you have the potential to unlock incredible insights and connections. Keep practicing, stay positive, and don't hesitate to explore new methods and refine your "clair" senses. The journey may be challenging, but the rewards are immense. You've got this!

Read on to Chapter 7 to learn about the ethics in animal communication and what your responsibilities are as a facilitator of any session, including practice sessions.

What We Learned in Chapter 6:

- A practical process to connect with animal consciousness, offering tips for beginners such as keeping detailed notes, embracing imagination, and practicing without pressure to distinguish genuine communication from your thoughts.

- Enhance animal communication by paying close attention to physical sensations (kinesthetic), practicing mental clarity to receive images (visual), and quieting the mind to hear subtle messages (auditory), noting all impressions for deeper understanding.

- Use an audio recorder to capture incoming information that is coming in quickly, trust the process, practice regularly, and believe in your ability to connect with animals; patience and persistence will lead to profound insights and improved skills.

CHAPTER 7

Ethics and Responsibility

A s we become more aware of the intricacies of animal communication, this exploration invites us to consider the responsibilities, boundaries, and moral decisions we face when engaging in nonverbal communication with animals. It's a space where we empower ourselves with knowledge and empathy, seeking to understand the ways in which our actions impact the vast web of life that surrounds us. This chapter encourages a nurturing approach toward all forms of communication, emphasizing the importance of ethical considerations in our interactions with the animal world.

The Importance of Ethical Practices

The field of animal communication is abstract and subjective, requiring a strong foundation in ethics. The "do no harm" principle is paramount as it ensures the welfare of the animal and cultivates a trusting relationship between the communicator, animal, and owner.

Special acknowledgment must be extended to my associate trainer, Kayla Gower, for her invaluable contribution to our ethical framework. Kayla coined the term "do no harm," which has become a foundational principle in our training programs and personal practices. This term eloquently encapsulates our commitment to nurturing and protecting the well-being of animals in all aspects of our communication.

ALEX ANDERSEN

"Do No Harm" Principles

- **Balance Honesty with Compassion:** Communicators must ensure that information from animals is conveyed truthfully while maintaining sensitivity to the emotions of both the animal and the owner.
- **Translate Animal Perspectives:** When interpreting messages, it's essential to not attribute human characteristics to the animals but to genuinely honor their perception and experiences.
- **Softening the Delivery:** It's important to share information gently, allowing the recipient to interpret the insights without causing harm. We should give the owner space for interpretation as they know their animal companion best and can provide valuable insight. This is especially important as we know that, as humans, we cannot be 100% accurate 100% of the time.
- **Highlight the Source of Information:** Recognize that the insights are based on the animal's perceptions, and this should be made clear to the caretaker.

Asking Permission

Consent is not only a fundamental ethical concern but also a foundational practice in animal communication. It respects the animal's autonomy and ensures transparency and respect in the communication process.

Seeking Consent

- **Domestic Animals:** Begin by asking permission from the caretaker and then the animal, making it clear that the consent of both parties is crucial.
- **Non-Domesticated Animals:** You must contact the animal directly to seek their consent. Don't worry; if they're not interested in talking, they simply won't answer!

- **Respect Any Refusal:** If an animal does not wish to communicate or express its boundaries by declining interaction, that choice should be respected without question.

Ethical Boundaries With Rescued Animals

Animals demonstrate an innate sense of their boundaries, particularly in their willingness to communicate. When animals choose not to disclose their past or feelings and the animal communicator does not press the issue, it doesn't mean that the animal communicator isn't doing their job. In fact, they are respecting the boundaries the animal has set. We must honor the animal's choice. Their silence can be a powerful message of self-preservation and a request for respect.

Our role is to offer support without force and to listen without demand. We must approach these beautiful beings with an open heart and a readiness to accept their terms of communication. If an animal is not ready to speak, we must respect their silence, support their presence in the current moment, and acknowledge their focus on healing and growth.

Present Over Past

Many rescued animals embody a profound lesson for us—that of living in the present. They often prioritize the present and the future over reliving their previous traumas. When they refrain from discussing their history, they may teach us the art of being deeply rooted in the now. It is an encouragement for us to help them focus on constructing a hopeful future rather than digging into a painful history.

This present-moment orientation displays animals' incredible resilience and solution-oriented nature. It's an invitation to foster their well-being by concentrating our energy on their healing and positive transformation.

Introducing Rescued Animals Positively

It is essential to be mindful of how we introduce our rescued companions to others. Refraining from defining them by their past traumas lays a foundation for their new identity. Our language and perspectives should empower them, celebrating their strength and capability to adapt and thrive.

Consider the difference in perception and energy when we introduce our rescued friends. A common introduction might go, "This is my dog, Chip. I rescued him from the pound, and he was pulled off the streets. I can't imagine what he had to go through to get here." While this statement is true, it centers Chip's identity around his past and rescue. It is also likely accompanied by low, sad, and concerned energy.

Compare this to a more empowering introduction, "This is Chip. He is the newest member of our family, and he has already grown so much since arriving. We are so proud to have him with us!" This approach celebrates Chip's progress and the bright future ahead of him rather than defining him by his past struggles. It's not just about semantics; it's about shaping perceptions and attitudes toward these remarkable survivors in a forward-thinking way. By choosing our words carefully, we nurture animals' dignity and support their integration into a new, happy, and fulfilled life.

Introducing them in their "most healed and whole state" not only offers an energetic benefit but also sends them telepathic affirmations of their valued place in our lives and their intrinsic worth beyond their history of rescue. This is by far more empowering than the latter.

Case Study: Holding Space for Healing

An impactful instance of honoring boundaries occurred during a session with a mare named Nova, who was rescued from a kill pen by a client of mine. After using Nova to birth babies for over half of her life, her old caretakers dropped her at the kill pen because she could no longer breed. Thankfully, my client was able to rescue her and bring her back to her ten-acre home to find healing and companionship.

During a session with Nova, she took some time to warm up to me. I was slow and gentle with her, letting her know I was there to give her a voice, that she was safe, and that we'd love to know what we could do to help her settle in and be more comfortable. Once she spoke up, she only communicated her need for space and her desire for basic necessities such as food and water. Even though everyone who participated in her rescue wanted to know more about her history, we recognized her requirements for space and that she did not want to talk about it. This boundary was respected, and she had nothing further to say, so we extended unwavering support to her and went to close the session.

I asked her if she was open to me checking in on her later, and she agreed. I followed up by asking her how long she needed until I checked back in, and she said about 30 days, or "one moon cycle." (With animals, sometimes, it is easiest to discuss time by discussing it in terms of the cycle of the moon.)

When I facilitated a session with her roughly 30 days later, she was in much better spirits. She still needed time to heal emotionally and physically, but she was finally open to discussing her needs with me! I asked her to paint me a picture of what she would consider to be her dream home.

This is always a helpful exercise for rescues for a multitude of reasons. First, it allows the caretaker to have invaluable insight into the desired environment for the animal, where it can heal and thrive. Second, it allows the animal to start dreaming of a positive future and gives them a sense of self and purpose. Nova expressed her desire for a loving home in nature where she could go on adventures. This insight led to finding her a perfect forever home, fulfilling her wishes for healing and happiness in the care of her human companion. Nova has since been incredibly happy and gets to go on lots of adventures.

After we granted Nova space and refrained from pressuring her, she eventually was ready to engage on her terms. The results demonstrate that true transformation happens in an environment that is safe, respectful, and supportive.

Every compassionate act that respects boundaries strengthens the ethical framework for our interactions with rescued animals, as well as animals of any background and circumstance. I would apply the rules above to any session: If the animal sets a boundary, it is my responsibility to respect that. This ongoing learning journey not only enhances the lives of the animals but also enriches our existence with them. It guides us through a collective path of healing, growth, and deep mutual respect.

In a traditional session, it's helpful for me to know the participants' intentions beforehand to ensure I'm ethically comfortable with the session's goal. For example, all the scenarios in this book fall within my comfort zone for animal communication sessions. However, occasionally, someone might push those boundaries. One key rule I emphasize to my students is to avoid communicating with an animal without permission or consent from the primary caretaker or owner. This could lead to ethical gray areas, such as asking invasive questions about the owner, which would not be appropriate. For instance, if a couple splits up and the pet moves to a different home, the person who no longer has the pet should not request an animal communication session to connect with that animal.

This approach is crucial, especially since the actual caretaker might be unaware of the session. We don't want to infringe on anyone's privacy or gather information that could harm relationships within the home. I would decline a session if someone asked to communicate with an animal without proper consent. Even if a trainer wants to communicate with an animal they are training, I typically require written or verbal consent from the owner. While these sessions can be valuable, it's essential to stay within ethical and professional boundaries by asking for permission.

I also always tell my students to constantly check ecology. Ecology is the practice of how something affects you and the environment around you; it is a study of consequences. Here's a list of ecology-based questions you might ask yourself before conducting an animal communication session if you are unsure if it is within your ethical bounds:

1. How will this affect me?
2. How will this affect those around me?
3. How will this affect society?
4. How will this affect the earth?
5. How will this affect the universe?

If you feel you're on firm ground after answering these questions, you are likely ready to move forward. I also ask myself these questions when I'm in an active session and am asked to cover certain topics that the animal might be reluctant to discuss.

If a questionable topic is brought up, such as the history of a traumatic past, I ask myself if this topic is solution-oriented. When animals choose to communicate about certain subjects like this, it's usually to address something unresolved and create solutions for it. Otherwise, their responses tend to be playful, fun, and focused on the present moment. I also consider the purpose and outcome of discussing a topic with an animal, ensuring it is constructive, positive, and yields the best results.

An interesting challenge arises when you're out in public and accidentally connect with an animal. This is common for those who practice animal communication regularly. As you improve, your unconscious mind may take over, much like muscle memory when riding a bike. You might find yourself unintentionally connecting with an animal without realizing it until you start receiving information from them.

This increased connection occurs because animals sense your skill level and vibrational openness, making them more attracted to you. However, it's still important to do your best to maintain ethical boundaries and only communicate with animals when you have permission and consent.

An Accidental Connection

I took Ginger to the vet one afternoon, and in the waiting room, I looked across the lobby and saw a beautiful black lab sitting across from us. As soon as my gaze met his, I accidentally became connected to him. The dog immediately said, "My mom's a nurse!" He stared and excitedly wagged his tail. I could feel how happy he was to be with her.

In a situation like this, I do not want to be impolite. I still want to respect the fact that it is always an honor for an animal to choose to communicate. However, that does not mean that it would be appropriate for me to have a full-blown conversation without the owner's knowledge.

In this situation, I looked over at the dog and politely and simply said, "That's great!" The dog replied, "Yes, I'm so proud of her." I told him how wonderful I thought that was and that I hoped they had a beautiful life together. Then I thanked him for sharing and disconnected.

You might wonder if I checked that the information was true, if the owner was, indeed, a nurse. While I was curious, pursuing that would have been my ego talking. Ethically, I always do my best to ensure I communicate with permission. So, I chose to politely acknowledge the dog, send love and support for their day, and then discontinue the connection.

To discontinue an accidental connection, use a method similar to intentionally creating one in an animal communication session. Visualize the energetic cord between you and the animal, which your unconscious mind created on autopilot, and then imagine cutting or removing this cord. Sometimes, I also look away and focus my attention elsewhere to avoid reconnecting accidentally.

Having a strong sense of energetic boundaries is going to be crucial as you build your skills. This is because if you do not have a strong sense of boundaries where you are able to turn the skill on and off, you will be met with lots of static chatter anytime you are surrounded by multiple animals. Just like most skills, this takes stamina. It also takes energy to facilitate this type of connection, especially for an ongoing amount of time. The longer you practice it, the more stamina you'll have to keep a connection for a longer period. So, don't be surprised while you are practicing if you can only hold and maintain a connection for five to ten minutes at a time. Continue practicing, and you will get stronger.

Once you have gotten pretty strong, it's time to build the on-and-off switch. I had to get very good at this because, at the beginning of my journey, I did not have a teacher telling me to practice energetic boundaries. So, I would go to places where there were lots of animals and become quickly overwhelmed by the chatter. In those spaces, it's very hard to pinpoint which animals are saying what to you, especially when there are five or more animals at a time.

Being able to turn off your communication skills is crucial for maintaining ethical boundaries. This reduces accidental connections and ensures you're not connecting when you can't help an animal, which can be problematic for them. For example, at events like dog shows, rodeos, or horse-riding competitions, accidental connections can happen. If an animal shares that they are in pain, you will likely be limited in your ability to do something about it. While sometimes we have the option to locate the owner and hope they are receptive to what we have to share, identifying and accessing the owner in such settings can be challenging. Even if you manage to share the information, the owner may not be open to hearing it, leaving you unable to help.

Another possibility that I would encourage you to be aware of is that sometimes, in a setting such as this, with many animals, we can sometimes pick up "telepathic static." This information could have come from almost anyone, and just because we think we may have accurately pinpointed where it did come from does not always mean that we're correct. Use your best judgment and proceed with caution.

Opening a line of communication with an animal without being able to assist them can create false hope for them, which is not fair. This goes against our principle of "do no harm." Only communicate with an animal when you have permission and can facilitate positive change.

Ultimately, our responsibility as animal communicators is rooted in love, a deep reverence for our craft, and a commitment to serving our communities. By adhering to these ethical standards, we honor the trust placed in us and ensure that our work is always in the best interest of the animals we seek to help. This dedication to proper ethics reflects our profound respect for the unique bond between humans and animals, guiding us to act with integrity and compassion in every interaction.

What We Learned in Chapter 7:

- Ethical practices in animal communication emphasize the "do no harm" principle, balancing honesty with compassion, honoring animals' perspectives, and seeking consent from both caretakers and animals to ensure transparency, respect, and the well-being of all involved.
- Respect the boundaries of rescued animals by honoring their choice to remain silent about their past, support their present-moment focus, and introduce them positively to others, emphasizing their progress and future rather than their past traumas.
- Before conducting an animal communication session, ensure it is within ethical bounds by asking ecology-based questions about the potential impact on yourself, those around you, society, the earth, and the universe.
- Respect accidental animal communication by acknowledging the animal briefly, ensuring the owner's permission is obtained for further interaction, and using visualization techniques to disconnect politely and ethically.
- Developing strong, energetic boundaries is essential for animal communicators to manage and control their skills, avoid overwhelming "telepathic static," ensure ethical practices, and only engage in communication when they can provide meaningful assistance.

CHAPTER 8

Real-Life Insights and Case Studies

In the realm of animal communication, every movement, sound, and silence is a part of a complex dialogue waiting to be understood. Through our compassion and willingness to listen, we can decode the messages that our animal companions strive to convey. This chapter is dedicated to sharing heartening real-life instances where understanding animal behavior led to transformational changes in the lives of the animals and their human counterparts. These stories are a celebration of empathy, patience, and the profound connections that develop when we choose to communicate with our entire being.

Case Study One: Cocaine, the Bucking Horse

Cocaine was a gelding whose history as a bucking horse had etched deep emotional scars. Shuffled from one home to another, his unpredictable episodes of bucking prevented him from finding permanent refuge. That is, until Margaret, with her nurturing heart, brought him under her wing. Despite previous owners' efforts and numerous medical evaluations that had ruled out pain as a cause, his troubling behavior under the saddle persisted. It was only when Margaret insisted on a thorough veterinary examination, including a scope, that the root of his distress was uncovered.

As Margaret narrated his journey to me, I could sense the turmoil within him. As she was chatting, he was sending me images and feelings of his stomach, all twisted up in knots as if full of acid. Due to my work as an animal communicator and with horses over many years, I immediately knew what the diagnosis was going to be. His actions weren't born out of mischief or stubbornness; they were desperate attempts to find relief from the severe pain of ulcers.

This often-overlooked medical issue, as I've come to find, leads to such undesirable behavior in many horses. Margaret's dedication to understanding the messages he was trying to convey through his behavior finally paid off for both of them. The decision to investigate his stomach issues exposed the harsh truth of his condition, but it marked the long-overdue beginning of Cocaine's path to recovery. It was Margaret's empathy and intuitive hit to dive deeper that became his beacon of hope, allowing him to heal and seek the peace he desperately needed.

The cherry on top of her intuitive hunches was recognizing the energy that must accompany the name Cocaine. Margaret decided a change was in order. She renamed him Tino, a name that better suited the calm and peaceful life she envisioned for him. The work had officially begun on his healing, both mentally and physically. Margaret sought my services to understand how Tino wished to spend his life moving forward.

In our sessions, Tino expressed his excitement about being with Margaret and his profound belief that they were meant to heal together. He conveyed his eagerness to be ridden again but asked to start slowly. Additionally, he showed an interest in tricks, indicating a desire for engagement and mental stimulation as part of his recovery process. The session was full of healing and understanding, and tears flowed with happiness for the possibilities on the road ahead.

Today, the two of them are still together. Shortly after our session, she shared a video of them working at liberty together. The love coming through was exuberant. Tino was calm and thrilled to be doing the "tricks" he'd been looking forward to.

Case Study Two: Theo's Plea for Attention

I came home to find an unexpected mess. One of my animals had urinated in a basket of newly cleaned clothes! Frustrated and puzzled after a long day of work, I stared at the basket, trying to figure out what could have been the cause of this choice. All my pets had been consistent with their bathroom habits, so the sudden change was out of the ordinary. Given that I had more than one pet, I couldn't immediately tell who was responsible for the incident. Was it a sign of illness, stress, or something else entirely?

With questions mounting and no clear answers, I decided to call an animal communicator for some insight. This was in the pre-stages of my animal communication phase, where I understood some things but still sought out the services of other animal communicators for assistance with my pets when I felt emotionally compromised. The communicator asked each animal until one finally fessed up. It turned out that Theo, my cat, was the one behind the unexpected behavior.

Theo quickly expressed that his actions weren't meant to cause trouble. Instead, they were a plea for attention. He shared that he was upset because of the long hours I had been working recently, which had left him feeling neglected and unseen, missing the quality time we used to spend together.

The message was clear: Theo longed for the companionship and interaction that had become scarce in our daily routine. Realizing this, I knew I had to make some changes. I reassured him that I would make more effort to be present and engage with him, a promise I intended to keep. I started carving out more time in my schedule for play and cuddles, even between meetings, making sure he felt valued and loved.

The efforts paid off. Our relationship became even better than before, and Theo's trust in me was renewed. He resumed his usual litter box habits, and our home life returned to normal. This experience served as a gentle reminder of the importance of being attentive to our pets' emotional needs and that sometimes, little slip-ups are simply expressing big emotional needs.

Case Study Three: Whiskey and the Mustang's Miscommunication

A client asked for a session regarding her horse, Whiskey. After having him for quite a while, he'd begun refusing the halter. Try as they might, he wouldn't let anyone catch him. This was a surprising new behavior for him.

In our session, Whiskey confessed an innocent but misguided belief implanted by his Mustang companions who had come off the range and were not yet halter trained. He said to me, "I was a rescue, and I want to stay. They told me that the trick to staying was not allowing people to catch them. If they can't catch us, we don't have to leave!"

While this is humorous, and I had to admit I understood the premise, the advice Whiskey had received was extremely misguided. Whiskey, having had numerous homes prior to this one, harbored a deep-seated fear of abandonment. With a simple conversation, I assured him that he was there to stay. To reengage him and make him feel seen, heard, and part of the family, I asked him, "What kind of job would you like here? What would be some of the things you'd really like to do?" He replied immediately, "I want to be the kid's horse!"

His request to become a cherished children's horse was fulfilled. Days later, my client sent me a photo of him happily haltered with her young boys and said he was a breeze to catch.

Case Study Four: Jack's Reflection of Unspoken Fears

Jack, a dog who stood in the shadow of legal reprimand, acted not from malice but as a mirror of his owner's unvoiced fears. When his owner called and shared that they were facing a court date due to a biting incident, I knew we were in for a few sessions together. I asked Jack why he had bitten the individual and the previous two, but he did not have an answer for me. All he could do was express his emotions at the time, the energy that had crept up in his body, and that he'd experienced a brief blackout like he didn't realize what he'd done until he'd come out of it.

Jack had no prior history of this type of behavior and no challenging past like some dogs I work with. This led me to the owner. Given that almost all of the biting incidents had been in public, I asked the owner how she felt out in public. She shared with me that she suffered from trauma and feelings of un-safety, mostly triggered when she was out in public. Jack's loyalty caused him to embody her inner turmoil, demonstrating the profound, often overlooked interconnectivity between human and animal emotions. He was simply mir-roring the projection of his owner's fears and inappropriately trying to protect her and himself.

With mutual acknowledgment of their shared vulnerabilities and the support of a professional trainer, we went to work. I taught Jack and his owner emotional release techniques to let go of the past and forge a new path for-ward. Their triumphant court appearance was not only a legal victory but also a personal triumph over their intertwined insecurities.

In the silent conversations we share with our animal companions, our energy speaks volumes, louder and clearer than any words could. The subtle-ness of our moods, the intensity of our thoughts, and the depth of our emotions create ripples in the environment, felt most acutely by those with whom we share our lives. Animals, with their innate sensitivity, become mir-rors to our soul's whispers, reflecting the energy we project, often without our conscious intent.

It's crucial, then, to become mindful of the energy we emit, focusing on projecting positivity, calm, and clear intentions. The essence of our commu-nication should pivot from what we aim to prevent to what we aspire to inspire within our animal companions—in other words, what we want rather than what we don't want. Verbal commands laced with frustration or fear can unknowingly cause them to be anxious or confused. Conversely, speaking from a space of love and certainty encourages understanding and mutual respect.

By harmonizing our internal landscape, we not only uplift our spirits but also help our animal friends feel secure and understood. The symbiotic flow of energy fosters an environment where drives and misconceptions fade, allowing for deeper, more meaningful connections to blossom.

Case Study Five: Nala, the Remarkable Gift of a Second Chance

Love is not just a feeling but an action, one that Nala desperately needed as she stood at the precipice of two paths. Misunderstood and branded a threat, her essence was clouded by the unwanted projections of fear from one of her owners.

When Nala's owners, Hal and Julie, called me, they shared that she was having aggression issues. Normally, when I facilitate such a session as this, it is to find workable solutions for all involved. However, quickly into the session, I realized that only Hal was interested in a solution. Julie had decided that Nala was no longer a good fit, so much so that she was convinced the only responsible thing to do about the aggression was to euthanize Nala.

I immediately began to ask more questions and found out that Nala had been found as a stray. Strays often pick up instinct-driven habits to help them fight and survive. It was my hunch that something was triggering this type of behavior with Nala. The owners shared with me that they'd had her for five years. When I asked when the behavior had begun, they just said within the last few years. I was shocked because, typically, if events from the past drive the behavior, it does not take this long to manifest. It had to be something else.

While chatting with them, Nala began to chime in my ear, sharing with me that she had never drawn blood. She was essentially trying to convey to me that she was not aggressive and that all her bites were warnings because she was scared. She was asking for help.

The owners confirmed this. Not only had she never actually successfully bitten anyone, but it only seemed to be an issue if they came up from behind her while she was sleeping. "Ah," I thought, "they're startling her, and she's scared."

To me, there were many possible solutions. However, Julie couldn't comprehend a world in which she might peacefully live with this dog without projecting fear onto her. In this type of environment, Nala would not get what she needed. Having an owner who would constantly project thoughts and pictures onto her about what she didn't want the dog to do versus what she did want the dog to do was setting Nala up for failure. The choice was made to re-home Nala. I facilitated the re-homing process, and Nala happily lived out the rest of her days with a loving owner who understood this principle. Not one single incident ever happened again.

Love is more than just an emotion; it's a commitment to action. These stories are odes to the depth and sincerity of an animal communication session. They remind us of the grace that exists when we resolve to not only listen but to understand, to provide solace, and to be the champions for those whose voices are spoken in a language without words. In recognizing these silent dialogues and discerning the subtle whispers of behavior, we liberate not only the animals around us but also our capacity for empathy and growth. Remember, the quest to connect with our animal companions is a shared journey. It enriches our lives and nourishes our souls.

As you continue to forge connections with the sentient beings around you, may you do so with an open heart and a listening spirit. May you find joy in every step, knowing that with each story of transformation, the world grows a bit kinder, a reflection of the nurturing bond that you cultivate with grace.

Conclusion

A nd so, we find ourselves at the close of our remarkable expedition together, one that has taken us through the intricate world of animal
communication and the profound connections it forges. From understanding
the subtleties of energetics to exploring the depths of the human mind with
its conscious and unconscious layers and the intricate dance between our neu-
rology and senses, we have explored a path of discovery and enlightenment.
Through practical exercises and digestible theory, you have learned to exercise the muscles of your mind and open your heart to the voices of these
amazing beings, exploring behaviors and messages that transcend the spoken
word.

Sessions on animal communication have unfolded common topics and
revealed the extraordinary outcomes of listening, truly listening, to the creatures with whom we share our world. This book's goal has been to kindle the
light of recognition within you that artful animal communication is not an
esoteric skill reserved for the few but a natural power within all of us. By deepening our understanding of ourselves, our animal companions, and the
environment we live in, we can make waves of positive change. When animals
and humans tap into this ancient yet innovative form of communication, we
pave the way for a more compassionate, understanding, and connected world.
Just imagine the strides we can make and the harmony we can co-create when
every one of us harnesses this innate ability.

As you stand at the threshold of new beginnings, brimming with newfound knowledge and insights, remember that this is not the end. Rather, it's an invitation, the first step into an expansive community that shares your passions and dedication. Whether you choose to join one of our comprehensive classes or mingle with like-minded souls in our free Facebook community, your journey has only just begun.

Our nurturing and empowering community is your haven, a space to further expand, grow, and transform, guided by compassion and shared vision. Here, you'll find the encouragement to tread boldly along your path of self-discovery and intuitive development, forging deeper animal bonds. This isn't merely a conclusion; it's a gateway to a future that's bright with promise, a world enriched by our collective awakening to the whispers of the natural realm.

Together, let us venture forward with our hearts open and minds attuned to the possibilities that await within the fold of animal communication. The world beckons. Will you answer the call? Join us and behold as the world transforms with one whisper, one insight, one connection at a time. We invite you to embark on a transformative experience by participating in our immersive and interactive classes.

Our live sessions provide a dynamic environment where you can practice and refine your newfound skills under the guidance of experienced mentors. In these classes, you'll have the opportunity to engage in real-time connections with animals, receive personalized support, and interact with a community of like-minded individuals who share your passion for animal communication. Through live demonstrations, exercises, and direct mentorship, you'll deepen your understanding and harness the power of telepathic communication in ways you never thought possible.

This is a journey of discovery, where you'll not only learn the art of animal communication but also cultivate a profound sense of connection and empathy. Together, we'll unlock the mysteries of interspecies communication and embark on a shared mission to honor and understand the voices of our animal companions.

Are you ready to take the leap and dig deeper into the extraordinary world of animal communication? Join our upcoming classes and become part of a vibrant community dedicated to nurturing the bond between humans and animals. Your journey toward profound connection awaits. Let's embark on this transformative plan together.

THANK YOU FOR READING MY BOOK!

DOWNLOAD YOUR FREE GIFTS

Don't forget, as a heartfelt thank you for reading our book, you can enjoy a complimentary training session to deepen your journey with animals!

Scan the QR Code:

SCAN ME!

I appreciate your interest in my book and value your feedback as it helps me improve future versions of this book. I would appreciate it if you could leave your invaluable review on Amazon.com with your feedback. Thank you!

Other Resources

Discover our signature 8-week course, featuring a proven and exclusive approach that you won't find anywhere else. Benefit from expert mentorship and personalized coaching, as you engage in live practices and receive targeted feedback while interacting with over 16 animals. This transformative experience uniquely enhances your skills and deepens your connection to animal communication, offering unparalleled insights beyond the pages of any book.

To Explore Upcoming Classes, Visit:

SCAN ME!

Unlock new levels of understanding and connection with your pet by partnering with a Certified Pet Talk Communicator, ensuring expert guidance and profound insights.

To Book With A Pet Talk Communicator, Visit:

SCAN ME!

www.ingramcontent.com/pod-product-compliance
Lightning Source LLC
LaVergne TN
LVHW041323080426
835513LV00008B/563